THE UNEXPECTED LIFE:
An Autobiography of a Very Human Priest

THE UNEXPECTED LIFE

An Autobiography of
a Very Human Priest

The Pastor Formerly Known as
Monsignor Dale Fushek

Published in the United States by Serey/Jones Publishers, Inc.
20118 N. 67th Ave Ste. 300-162
Glendale, AZ 85308

ISBN: 978-1-881276-05-0

Web site: www.theunexpectedlife.com

TABLE OF CONTENTS

THE UNEXPECTED LIFE: An Autobiography of a Very Human Priest

FOREWORD
BY JODY SEREY

The truth is I have known Dale Fushek for so many years I can't quite remember how or when we were thrown together for the first time. However, I know our meeting was related to the publishing company that we both worked for back in the halcyon days of post-Vatican II optimism and idealism. We were both unbelievably young and energetic.

Dale was a brand-new priest, with the seminary just barely behind him. We found in each other common values, shared interests, and a belief in the staying powers of friendship. When I married David Serey, Dale urged me to make the marriage right with the Catholic church. So I sought an annulment from my first marriage, and was eventually granted one by the tribunal.

Dale married David and me as Catholics, and eventually

when we adopted our three children, he made his way three separate times through the stacks of paperwork required to establish our credentials as people of character good enough to parent. He baptized each child as soon as it was legally permissible to do so, and I kept him supplied somewhat sporadically with school pictures and the like. We thought the logistics of our lives were getting complicated. In retrospect, we didn't appreciate how simple they actually were.

Some years passed when we barely saw each other, and depended on a card or a note to verify that each was still alive. His career took off like a bottle rocket, and my life became a decidedly secular tangle of family issues, corporate calisthenics, and suburban insensitivity. I never became part of the parish that he led for 20 years, and his address on the other side of the town sometimes seemed very far away indeed.

So there are many others who could rightfully claim that they know Dale better, are closer to him, and hold the secrets of his heart. I would be hard put to argue any of that, even if challenged to do so. However, we have survived more than three decades of ups and downs, and aging. It is good to look into the face of a long-time friend and still see what I consider to be the "real me" reflected back. Dale still knows me. For this I am grateful, because the stage props and the costuming have all changed a great deal.

Many years ago I had a moment of absolute clarity when I realized that the defining truth of my life is the phrase, "And this, too, shall pass." Dale quoted these words earnestly and often, and we all believed because we were young and filled with fervor that they indicated that evil goes away, is banished eventually, and hits the proverbial fast track back to hell. It never occurred to us — not a single time — that the meaning is one size fits all, and that it also applies to the good things in life.

In the late 1980s, I had the occasion to share a few fleeting moments with Mother Teresa. Just beyond the room where we stood, an enormous cheering crowd was assembled on her behalf. Donations in the form of cash, checks, and canned goods almost literally rained down like manna from heaven. As she emptied the pockets of her little sweater and handed back fistfuls of money to me, I said to her, "Mother, isn't this wonderful?"

She turned to me, and looked me right in the eyes with the slightest of smiles. She nodded and said very quietly, "It is wonderful. And it will also all change."

I was shocked, but said nothing. I knew the meaning of her remark. "And this, too, shall pass."

Her words didn't haunt me, but they did do something much more invasive. They became an echo inside my head. I took them as a generic warning that there was always another shoe – or in some cases, another sandal – to be dropped. And when it did drop, it did so with the crash heard round the world. Or sadly in some cases, it was more like a snicker.

The priest sex scandals became the fodder of smirking monologues made by overpaid late night television hosts. Even as the lives of both the guilty and the innocent were being forever changed, pedophile priest jokes took their place alongside quips about Michael Jackson, O.J. Simpson, Robert Blake, and other media targets. In Arizona, newspapers both large and small presented enough sensationalism to line the bottoms of bird cages for millennia.

When I first heard Dale's voice on the national news, he was testifying at the trial of Bishop Thomas J. O'Brien who was accused of leaving the scene of a fatal accident. I was quite familiar with hearing Dale's voice on CNN, as he was often consulted about one major Catholic church event or the other, including the ongoing investigation into the misconduct of priests. However, his voice and demeanor were very different when he addressed the questions posed by the attorney regarding the bishop. I could tell that under his Roman collar, Dale was a man whose throat was tight with grief.

When allegations of a sexual nature began to be hurled against Dale, my first reaction was disbelief. I said to my dinner companions in the small café in northern Arizona where the television droned the evening news and I first learned of the ordeal that was now Dale's, "I know this man very well. He didn't do these things."

That is still my stance, even though Dale has been exonerated by expert polygraph testing and the general unraveling of the accusations against him. Mine is not just the knowledge and wisdom of the heart – it's based on firsthand observation over many, many years.

I know this man very well. He didn't do these things.

In the midst of the media feeding frenzy that ensued, and a series of newspaper articles that should have been packaged in plain brown wrappers, I sent Dale a note that said, "What can I do to help?"

He called and answered, "Help me write a book. We've written books together before. But this one will be different."

We met regularly for months, and I heard his confession. He remained unflinching, straightforward, and candid. As the time passed and resolution of a sort was reached, I sensed less despair and more hope, and more genuine peace of mind than resignation. We have always afforded each other a certain amount of privacy, a particular safety zone of personal space. So I don't pry, or try not to. But I think he has found the world outside the Catholic church to be both terrifying and wonderful, and his relationships beyond the rectory to be filled with dignity and reassurance. He is finding ways to balance the profane with the truly sacred.

We finished each meeting with a ritual bowl of soup, and I marked the weeks by the simple meal and the unhurried conversation. I remain convinced that my long-time friend is one of the true gifts of my life, and I will always love him.

This is something that will not pass, even though time – and eventually we who mark it – inevitably will. Love is eternal.

Jody Serey, Fall 2010

PREFACE

We all remember the story of Forrest Gump. His whole life was made up of unique and incredible experiences. Although we know that his life was a work of fiction, we were willingly drawn in to his adventures. I do not pretend that my life is quite so interesting. But, my years as a Catholic priest have been filled with spiritual and mundane adventures, good and bad, that I NEVER expected. I am writing this book to share my life with you. It is my hope that you will receive insight into the priesthood, to me, and to the hand of God.

The greatest experiences of my life are people. Not just some of the famous ones that I mention in this book, but friends and people of faith who have shared themselves with me. I am humbled by the simple and deep faith of parishioners. I am inspired by the Mark Keoughs (my best buddy) of the world who are trying to live faithfully. There have been many individuals — friends, co-workers, Life Teen Board Members, young people, and families

— who have been the face of God for me. I am very grateful for them all.

The worst experiences of my life are people. These are folks who craft lives of anger, accusations, and greed. There is no doubt that the world, the Catholic church, and my life have been cluttered with the presence of toxic people in addition to the terrific people I mentioned.

My vocation traces back to my high school days. I always thought I would marry my great friend Pam (who is now a judge). One day, while working at a local grocery store, I was approached by the vice president of the chain, the divisional manager, and the store manager about entering management training.

My response was "I can't sell liquor." I was only 17. They thought I was graduating from college, not high school.

That night, I lay in bed trying to sleep. For some reason, I asked myself what I wanted to do with my life. I tried to picture myself on my deathbed and imagine what I would have accomplished. I realized that night what was important to me was not money, or success. I wanted to learn how to LOVE.

Therefore, I have sought love. I have sought to understand it and to teach it. I have gone halfway around the world to Yugoslavia (Medjugorje) where I heard that the Blessed Mother was appearing. I hoped to see love face-to-face with Mary. While in Medjugorje I met young people who were seeing apparitions of Our Lady.

One of the most moving things I heard there was that people were beautiful because they loved and people who hated were ugly and miserable. The lack of peace in the world came from the lack of love. After that trip, I wanted to love even more deeply. Traveling to Yugoslavia changed my life.

I believe that the desire to love was the passion of my heart. I believe it still is! And, I am trying to see my journey in this light.

It's not easy. I have failed so many times and in so many ways. I have also experienced the faithfulness of God's love over and over again.

In this book, I did not "spiritualize" everything. My intent is neither to inspire Catholics, nor discourage Catholics or non-Catholics. My intent is to share HONESTLY one man's journey in learning how to love.

I hope that whoever reads this book, whether a person of faith or not, sees in the death and resurrection of his or her own life, the incredible power of love, and the incredible journey of all who seek it.

To my family — especially my mom, Jeanne, my sister, Lyn, and my brother, Dean — my friends, and my brothers and sisters in faith, I say THANK YOU for loving. For those who read this book, THANK YOU for sharing life with me.

Dale Fushek, Fall 2010

THE UNEXPECTED LIFE: An Autobiography of a Very Human Priest

CHAPTER 1
UNEXPECTED EXPECTATIONS

I always thought it was funny when families with children came up to me after church, and a little kid asked "Are you God?" or "Are you Jesus?"

I always responded, "No, but I work for him." Or, "He's a friend of mine."

To a little kid, when I was dressed up and everybody was listening to what I had to say, I appeared to be somebody important.

If one is a priest, parents want their kids to be hugged by you or acknowledged by you in some personal way. I think in general people have high expectations of and for their priests.

I remember once when I was pushing a cart through a grocery store I met a woman parishioner who was shopping with her little boy. We stopped to talk for a few minutes, and when I walked away I heard the little boy say, "Mommy, who is that?"

His mother said, "That's Fr. Dale from church. You know who he is."

And the boy said, "Sure. He's the king."

She asked, "Honey, what do you mean he's the king?"

And the little boy explained that he had seen a movie where the king entered a room, and the people all stood up. The king also sat on a throne, and wore fancy robes, and everybody listened to what he had to say.

I think to many very young people, and even to some older people, a priest seems like a power person, some sort of ruler. And yet as a priest I don't think I ever recognized the kind of power that I carried, and the position carried, in terms of influencing people, or causing people to try to please me or get my attention.

A good friend of mine named Peggy Redman said to me shortly after I arrived at St. Timothy's, "Fr. Dale, there are two kinds of power – position power and personal power. And I'm telling you now, if you want to be a good pastor, don't use position power. Don't just say we're going to do things this way because I'm the pastor and I say so. Don't say that's the way it is because I say that's the way it is. You need to use personal power, your charisma, to draw people into your vision."

What I tried to do as a priest was to have a vision as to what the parish, the Catholic church, or the world could be and draw other people into it. I think one of the problems in the Catholic church today is that a lot of the priests don't have any vision, and they don't have any personal power. So they use a lot of position power to force their viewpoints on the people they are serving. This approach often works well to maintain the status quo, but it does nothing to grow the church or to deepen people's faith lives.

Regardless, whether it's position power or personal power or charisma, even a priest is still just a sinner. We're just ordinary guys.

I have repeated those exact words to people. "I'm just a guy."

That old saying about putting your pants on one leg at a time is true. You're just a guy who has likes and dislikes. There are people in the parish you really like and would like to get to know. And there are other people who have different personalities and grate you the wrong way. It's the real world even inside a rectory, and you're part of the human race. Yet people have the expectation that since you're a priest, you don't have feelings. You don't possess vulnerabilities.

I remember that shortly after I came to St Timothy's a man approached me after a Life Teen mass. He had fire in his eyes and he said, "I'm Lt. Col. So-and-So of the United States Air Force, and what I saw in there tonight was shameful. It was the worst disgrace I have ever seen in the church. It was all about you. I didn't appreciate you using humor. I didn't like the music. It was an absolute disgrace."

Being the shy person that I am, I came right back at him. "Sir, I'm sorry that you feel that way, but you are a disgrace to your uniform. There is no lieutenant colonel in the United States Air Force who would walk up to a superior officer and talk to him or her the way you just spoke to me. So you, sir, are a disgrace to our country."

This was an absolute use of position power. I was essentially saying, "You can't talk that way to me" instead of finding out what was really going on with him.

About 10 years later the same man walked up to me after mass and he said, "I'm Lt. Col. So-and-So."

I said, "I remember you."

He answered, "You do? Well, I just wanted to apologize. I have been watching you for a number of years and what is going on here is amazing. So I just wanted to let you know I'm sorry for what I said those years back."

Religion is a very deep experience for each of us and we have individual feelings based on how we grew up, what kinds of people we are, what our parents were like, and what the name "father" means to us personally. These factors strongly influence what our expectations are.

When you go into a public environment such as a restaurant or a sporting event and you are wearing a Roman collar, nobody knows how to deal with you. On some level, almost everybody is uncomfortable.

I remember going to the Dove Awards in Nashville – the Christian music awards – and I was wearing a Roman collar. They let me into all the secure places where supposedly only top security was allowed. They didn't want to say no to a priest.

I have had the experience, as have most priests, of being in a restaurant and signaling for the bill only to be told by the server, "Oh, your bill was already taken care of, Father. Somebody took care of it before they left."

I have also had the experience of going with the bishop to a high school that was to be closed, and being spit on by a student. So I experienced that side of the Roman collar, too.

I had a parent grab me the night we went to close the school, and I was afraid he was going to punch me. He said, "I used to respect you, but I don't respect you any more."

One time I was in a store shopping for an anniversary gift for my parents and a man came up to me and said, "You shouldn't even be in here. You should be out serving the poor."

But if you think that's bad, you should see people's reactions when you come out of the bathroom. They just sort of stare as if to say, "Oh my God, when did they start doing that? Vatican II has just changed everything."

People just don't understand you. You're different, and they want you to be different, but they don't want you to be different. They have all kinds of expectations, and somehow they think you came from the Holy Family – that your dad and mom are Joseph and Mary, and you just sort of dropped out of heaven in a celestial Glad Bag. You're not allowed to be part of the human race. In truth, you're an ordinary guy from an ordinary family with ordinary problems.

A priest is someone who heard a call and is trying to serve. I think when you're a young priest, people are excited for you and enthusiastic, but after a few years the glow sort of fades. Folks treat you differently when you're a middle-aged priest, and they certainly treat you differently when you're an old priest.

Perhaps all aging people are treated differently and it doesn't really matter what profession you're in. But I believe it is especially true for clergy.

My biggest fear about becoming a priest was becoming an old priest. We all remember the words from the Beatle's song Eleanor Rigby. People are usually kind to old priests, but older priests are very isolated and lonely.

Clergy deal with a lot of negativity. That gets exaggerated, at least in my experience, because there are people who like the changes in the Catholic church, and people who don't. In a sense, it's like being a politician.

Politicians live in extreme negativity. You can be riding the wave of popular sentiment at one moment, and crashing the next. But the payoff for a politician has to do with money, position, power, prestige, and those kinds of things. For a priest, many of those elements can exist, too, but there is no financial payoff. There's a real security issue.

So the negativity that is absolutely a part of the human condition is absolutely part of the experience of being a priest.

In my experience people have high expectations because people have high needs. Families are needy. Women who are not being heard by their husbands come to the priest to be listened to. Maybe it's in confession. Maybe it's in counseling.

Men who don't have friends or buddies want that kind of relationship with the priest.

People have high needs. As families break up and many people turn to their churches for comfort, they can have extremely high expectations.

At the same time, Americans bring into our experience the whole dynamic of church consumerism. Unlike in the past, church membership is not dictated by where one lives. People seek out the place where they will be fed. For better or worse, people become consumer conscious when it comes to the Catholic church, and they seek out what they need regardless of where they actually reside.

This puts a lot of pressure on a priest as pastor. It is assumed that he is going to be a good business person, a good fundraiser, and a good preacher. He is also supposed to be gentle, compassionate, and available in the middle of the night if there is a crisis. He is expected to be able to rejoice if somebody is getting married and weep when somebody dies and a family is grieving. He is also supposed to be able to hire and fire staff in a very professional manner.

These are skills that no priest ever trained for. There is no seminary degree for these abilities.

For several years, I was a guest speaker in the business department of Arizona State University. Ironically, I had never taken a single business class in my life. I was never even shown how to operate a mimeograph machine, much less a copier or a computer. However, none of that prevented me from waking up one day to discover that I was running a corporation with 120 employees and a $6 or $7 million dollar budget.

As a result of me becoming the unwitting CEO of a corporation, I was asked to come speak to a college level business class about running a non-profit organization. I went in all prepared, and ready to fend off whatever questions the students hurled at me. I had a diagram and a flow chart of how the parish operated in relationship to the diocese, and to the universal church.

The first question a student posed was, "What is your mission statement?"

I asked, "The mission statement of the Catholic church?"

She replied, "Yes. We learned that you never start a business without creating a mission statement."

It was an epiphany to me. I answered, "The mission statement of the Catholic church was given to us by our founder Jesus when he said after the resurrection, 'Go and baptize all nations.' That's our mission statement."

We are called to go – not sit – so we are called to action. We are called to baptize, or immerse, or dip. Go dip all nations. Our mission statement encompasses everybody – all age groups, divorced people, separated people, gay and straight people, African American, White, Hispanic, Native American – it doesn't matter. The mission statement of the Catholic church is to go immerse the entire world and every aspect of people's lives into the water of life, Jesus Christ.

Obviously, it is an impossible mission statement. And obviously no one person can do it. Some of us have tried. Some are still trying, with varying degrees of success. Yet even trying is an incredible experience.

Families also present a common list of expectations to their priests. Working moms, stay-at-home moms, and parents in general deal with the needs of their children in terms of religious education, all of which require specific support from their priests.

But despite the seemingly endless demand that I submerge my life into other people's daily existences, I have learned that in America there are two areas that people don't want to immerse into anything, including Jesus. They don't want their priest near their sex lives and they don't want them near their finances. And when a priest addresses those areas of their lives, he either gets the reaction of "Stay out of my pocket!" or "Stay out of my bedroom!" or he may hear, "Wow. Thank you. Now I understand what this about. This is about surrendering all of my life to God."

As a priest, I instruct people not to take control, not to win, not to be competitive, but to surrender their lives to the will of God and to live their lives in ways that are pleasing to God. And all the time I am saying the words, I know that I am struggling to do these things, too. Everybody struggles to surrender to the will of God – even His own son.

I have met saints who have struggled with it every day of their lives. After her death, it was revealed that Mother Teresa dealt with depression. People were very quick to say, "See? She wasn't such a saint after all, was she?"

Quite the contrary. What defines somebody as holy is that when the odds are against him or her, or temptation is there, that he or she continues to strive to please God. This is also similar to the definition of courage — feeling the fear and doing what has to be done anyway.

That is also what sanctity is about, too — feeling the temptation and choosing to do the right thing. Or not choosing to do the right thing, then choosing to accept mercy and forgiveness. It takes surrender to accept mercy from God. Truly, what it takes to be a priest is to be open to the work of the Holy Spirit.

One day I went to lunch with Pat Kruska from our parish staff, and when we returned and were about to walk through the doors of the church, a pickup truck pulled up and a man yelled out, "Father, help me."

I turned to the woman I was with and told her to go ahead. I then walked over to the truck to talk to the driver, and saw that he had a gun pushed into his stomach. He said he was going to kill himself. My pleasant lunch hour evaporated as quickly as that.

I started talking to the man, feeling nervous for him, nervous for me, and definitely nervous in the presence of the gun. But I didn't want him to drive away because he wasn't stable and I was afraid he would hurt himself, or somebody else. I did everything I could to engage him in conversation, and to encourage him to stay.

As we talked, I actually slid my hand between the barrel of the gun and his stomach. I said, "Maybe you should just put that gun down because you aren't going to shoot my hand off." Even as I said the words, I doubted them.

My secretary came outside to look for me because my next appointment was waiting. I turned around and mouthed to her, "Call the police."

She went back inside very quietly to dial 911, and within a few minutes the entire complex was surrounded and the church parking lot was blocked off. There was a SWAT team on the church roof, and officers with rifles were perched everywhere.

I was relieved to see the officers, but I was also concerned that the man in the truck might have his death wish fulfilled. It's not uncommon for an emotionally distraught person to commit what is called "suicide by cop." A lot of desperate people choose to die at the hands of somebody else. I was certain that was what I was witnessing.

Suddenly, the man's cell phone rang. It was on the dash of the truck. I said to him, "Shouldn't you answer your phone?"

And he said, "No. I already know who it is. It's my mother."

I asked, "Then can I answer it?"

He didn't say anything, so I reached over and picked it up and said, "Hello?"

A woman's voice said, "Who is this?"

So I said, "Who is this?"

She told me her name, and said she was the man's mother. She wanted to know if her son was all right, and I said that I was with him but that he was having some troubles. I also said that I hoped that he would allow us to get him some help.

She asked who I was, and I said, "This is Father Dale."

There was a pause, and she started to cry. She said she was in the Midwest, and she had been sitting alone praying that her son would go see me. He had called her, and it was obvious to her that he wasn't well, but she knew nobody in Phoenix and didn't know how to advise him to seek treatment. However, she had seen me on television on EWTN, and she had urged her son to find out where I was and go to me for help.

After more reassurances, the man gave me a gun and I tossed the gun to the police. Nobody was hurt, and the man was hospitalized.

Sometimes, that is the way the Holy Spirit works. It arrives unbidden and unexpected, and you have to do the best you can to answer the call. It still amazes me that the Spirit works through me – and through you – although we are sinners and imperfect vessels. It is also amazing how many more times the Holy Spirit could work if we didn't close the door because of fear or an unwillingness to leave the comfort of our own lives.

It is sometimes exciting living and working in a rectory. We were broken into by a would-be burglar, and the little cocker spaniel I had bit the intruder. Bishop O'Brien said he was going to make the dog a monsignor since he was such a tireless defender of the faith.

I have had threats against my life. There was a time at another parish where I answered a call to help arbitrate a domestic dispute, and a fight. A huge man who had been drinking was not glad to have me summoned, and he armed himself with a lamp he was going to throw. I walked in and ordered him, "You, put that down."

To my immense relief, he did. This guy could have eaten me for lunch, but I think I scared him and he calmed down somewhat. The family and I got him into rehab where he could get counseling, and I went home at about 6:00 a.m. As I lowered my weary body into bed, the phone rang and a voice on the other said, "Where is he?"

I repeated, "Where is he? Where is who?"

The voice said, "You know who I mean. Where did you put him?"

I played dumb and said, "I really don't know what you're talking about."

The voice said, "I know where the rectory is, and I know which room is yours. And if you don't tell me, you'll be dead in a half hour."

I hung up on the caller, and then I dialed the 911 operator. The operator said, "Don't mess around with that," and she put me through to the police.

The police officer asked, "What do you want us to do? Is he there?"

I said, "No. But can you send an officer out to look around and make sure he isn't here?"

An officer was dispatched, but found nothing. I never heard another word from the mystery caller, but the entire incident certainly drove home the point to me that rectory life wasn't what I had expected it to be. It could often be lonely, but it was seldom ever quiet.

The human encounters rolled by, one after another. Late one night I returned from making a sick call. When I got to the rectory there was a man leaning over a car in the parking lot. I drove by and parked my car in the garage, and I thought of the story of the Good Samaritan and I was ashamed that I hadn't stopped to ask if he was okay. I thought I had better go check on him.

When I returned, I found him with his pants down around his ankles and he was masturbating against the car. His wallet was on the hood of the car, and the contents were all spread around, minus money and credit cards. He was in his early 20s, and he was completely intoxicated – totally oblivious to me or anything around him.

What had happened is that he had gone out with some people he thought were his friends, and he had gotten high and drunk. His friends emptied his wallet and went off and left him. Fortunately, his driver's license was still there, so I locked up his car and put him in my car and drove him home.

God puts people like that in your way, under the most undignified and vulnerable conditions. It's certainly something I never anticipated encountering as a part of my ministry.

My very first night at St. Timothy's, I got an obscene phone call. The person had the numbers for all three parish lines, and as I hung up one line he would call the next one. His fury and his venom were as ferocious as his profanity, and I finally resorted to hanging up.

The priesthood is an interesting life. I'm not saying others don't have interesting lives, but I can certainly tell you that mine has been fascinating. If a man is a priest, people want him to live somehow differently than they are living, but at the same time they want him to live like they are living so he will understand them and remain in touch with what they are feeling.

They want him to not be married, but to understand marriage. They want him to not be a parent, but to understand parenting. They want him to not be a sinner, but to understand the need for mercy.

I think that these mutually exclusive expectations are all part of the struggle of the priesthood. It's a life of conflicts.

A priest is called to something that is very, very difficult to live. And at the same time there are people who want him to live it perfectly and want that example to guide their own lives. Sadly, there are also people who want the priest to fall.

I have had more than one woman say to me, "I understand your needs, and I will take care of them. Nobody will ever know."

As a priest, you are a powerful figure to them, and temptations are there. And certainly as a priest you can take advantage of people because they want to be very good to you. It is not difficult to abuse the goodwill of people who want to please you.

I have been blessed with some very wonderful friends. I could never have afforded to go to the Super Bowl, yet I have been to the Super Bowl because of the Bidwill family's thoughtfulness. I could never afford to take some of the trips I've taken, but I've been many places because of people's kindness. People do want you to be part of their family, and part of their experience.

But somehow the expectation is that you're in touch with them, and you're above where they are. Somehow you're going to raise other people up to a higher level just by being among them. But the truth of the matter is, there are other people in the parish who may not have the formal spiritual training that you have as a priest, but who spiritually are far beyond where you are because of their ability to surrender to God.

I believe that as a pastor I am called to heal, to challenge, to forgive, and to accept people. There was a young man who was a teenager at the time and who was having sex with his girlfriend. I can recall the exact bench I sat on at the parish to talk to this kid. I was all over him in my righteous indignation, saying things like "Dude, what are you doing? You shouldn't be doing that."

This 17-year-old kid looked me square in the eye and said, "You know what? I am not going to stop. And if you want to love me and accept me, I will be honest with you and we can be friends. And if you don't want to, then that's up to you."

I remember being so taken back that he had the wisdom and the guts to answer me as he did that I just looked at him and said, "Well, I do love you and I will still love you." And 20 years later, he was still somebody I counted as a great and true friend.

I didn't always agree with what he did. I don't agree with what a lot of people do. But I have learned that I just have to accept people and realize that each person is more than one act, more than one decision. You accept the goodness in other people.

For me, that was the ultimate challenge. How did I as a priest accept people as they were, love people as they were, yet stand for what I believe? And at the same time, how did I call people to be holier than I was myself?

When I verbalized this, some people thought it was hypocritical. And in a sense, I suppose it could be looked at that way. Yet what father doesn't want his children to be happier than he is? That is the nature of being a father.

I take the term "father" very, very seriously — maybe sometimes too seriously. I discovered long ago that I was called to father — to set a whole spirit of shepherding — for an entire community. There were hundreds and thousands of people who experienced me, their priest, as a spiritual father and felt my shepherding with all its imperfections.

As you will read, especially in the later chapters, the unexpected events of my life became far more bizarre than I ever could have imagined. My life, including giving up the priesthood, caused incredible pain. But through it all, I have come to expect the UNEXPECTED. And, I've also learned to EXPECT the extraordinary and constant love of an amazing father.

Every pastor is a sinful human being, but he still has the vocation and the responsibility of being a father to thousands of people. Young, old, weak, strong, Catholic, and non-Catholic – they represent every walk of life, and bring with them every good and bad experience from a multitude of existences. Yet a priest is just one man. He's just an ordinary guy trying to do an extraordinary job for a Savior who bought our lives with a perfect sacrifice.

And believe me, some days are better than others.

CHAPTER 2
POPE JOHN PAUL II

What we all watched on television upon the death of Pope John Paul II was something magnificent. Four million people showed up for his funeral, which was probably one of the largest funerals ever in history. It is my understanding that the president of Italy called the president of Poland and said, "Don't let anybody else come. The city is full."

Rome was filled to capacity. The streets were jammed with people, and thousands waited in line 12 to 18 hours just to file past the pope's body. But despite the crowds, it was a respectful, peaceful gathering. One has to wonder what there was about this man that touched so many people.

He certainly redefined the papacy. He temporarily put a loving, human face on the Catholic church. He also taught us how to live, and he showed us what it is to die without fear and with dignity.

Certainly Pope John Paul II will be regarded as one of the great figures of the 20th and 21st centuries. Pope Benedict XVI waived the five-year waiting period to begin canonization of John Paul, so that process has already started largely in response to the widely held belief of people all over the world that there was something truly remarkable about him.

It is said that John Paul had the most recognized face in the world and was the most photographed person in history. This undoubtedly had to do with the amount of traveling he did, how present and available he was to the media, and how well he understood the potential of the media for reaching people. He used them in the most positive sense, and they responded with a level of deference that almost nobody else is afforded today.

As were many other people, I was graced with the privilege of being able to see John Paul in person in Denver in 1993 at World Youth Day, in Toronto in 2002 at World Youth Day, and in Rome in 2000. I also saw him in 1982 and 1995 during pilgrimages I made to Rome. Whenever I was where he was, even though there might be a half million or even a million other people around me, I still felt his presence and his strength.

I was also blessed to have two personal encounters with John Paul, and the experience both times was unforgettable. The first was in 1987 during his pastoral visit to the United States when I had the opportunity to coordinate the mass at Sun Devil Stadium. The second time was in 1995 in Rome.

In Phoenix in 1987, I coordinated two ceremonies – one at Ss. Simon and Jude Cathedral, an ecumenical prayer service. The second was the papal mass held at Sun Devil Stadium at Arizona State University in September. The stadium usually held about 70,000 people, but we added 10,000 seats on the field, so the final nose count was 80,000. Mercifully, it was cool for the desert at that time of the year, or some of those 80,000 noses might have ended up face down. We were very lucky with the weather.

We had heard a lot of jokes about the pope celebrating mass at Sun "Devil" Stadium, and there was such concern that we covered up the little devil mascots for Arizona State so they wouldn't offend anybody's sense of dignity. In the end, the stadium proved to be an almost ideal venue for the papal mass, and all things considered, everything went together almost flawlessly. Almost.

Two years before in 1985, I had been called into Bishop Thomas O'Brien's office, and the bishop said, "Guess who's coming to dinner?"

I said, "Oh, I don't know. The pope?"

The bishop replied, "How did you know?"

I said, "I didn't know. I was just kidding."

The bishop continued, "There is a chance he will be here," and then he assigned my dear friend and goddaughter, Marge Injasoulian, and me to the task of coming up with a proposal as to why the pope should come to Phoenix. We had 48 hours to complete everything, and to make the presentation.

We got statistics, information, and all kinds of data we thought would lend emotional weight to our side, and made the presentation to a representative of the United States Catholic Conference of Bishops. Ultimately it was decided that the pope would come here for a visit with a dual focus on health care (because of St. Joseph's Hospital) and on Native Americans.

I went to New York with Sr. Anthony Poerio of the diocese's Office of Worship to begin preparations. We had two years to pull together one of the most logistically and liturgically complicated tasks that we would ever face.

Papal liturgy is an entity unto itself. The details you have to pay attention to are endless –where the server walks, what bishop is in line where, who sits where, and so forth. The scope of it is absolutely incredible.

19

Security was also a huge concern. Therefore, the two areas that I became most involved in were the liturgy and security. We met with the Secret Service for two years straight. I remember how amiable and personable the Secret Service personnel were at the early meetings, and how enjoyable it was to get to spend time with people in their profession. However, as the event drew closer, they lost their sense of humor and their approachability. Two years out, everybody was friendly and relaxed. As the time drew for the papal mass drew near, the Secret Service got super intense. For that matter, we all did.

When the day of the papal mass arrived, we ran into some really potentially serious trouble. The metal detectors that had been sent out of San Antonio had been caught in a hail and windstorm and weren't working right. So the lines of people being admitted to the stadium became delayed, and backed up. We eventually resolved the problem, but we had momentary visions of almost 80,000 very frustrated people locked out of the stadium and the pope appearing before a lot of bleachers and folding chairs.

Meanwhile, a friend of mine was coordinating all the communion arrangements. You must remember that giving communion to 80,000 people is a gargantuan task and all the Vatican permits is less than 20 minutes to do it. But the Secret Service would not give the volunteer the security clearance to do what he needed to do to make sure that everything went smoothly, and in a liturgically correct manner.

The Secret Service had provided all those involved with the papal liturgy little color-coded pins, and the color of the pin determined how close the wearer could get to the Holy Father. The pin that my friend had been given permitted him access to the back stage area, but not total access.

We had 80,000 communion hosts counted out and put into beautiful baskets that the Native Americans had made, and that morning the bomb sniffing dogs went through and knocked over hundreds of the baskets. So the communion hosts that were carefully allotted for each section were in total disarray.

But as the hosts were being sorted out again, my friend found a little pin on the ground whose color indicated to the Secret Service that the wearer was an armed guard. So he just put on that pin, and from then on he had access to wherever he wanted to go to be sure that communion came through right on schedule, which it did. We didn't consider it a genuine breech of security – more like divine intervention.

With all the precision involved in the arrangements we made or others made for us, the human element persevered. In fact, one of the most human elements involved the trailer we had set up for the pope to use to dress, or vest, and to attend to his personal needs. We soon discovered that we had forgotten to provide him with some fruit, and with toilet paper.

The toilet paper was a particular problem because we had to send the Secret Service out of the enclosed area to get what they call a stadium roll – which has a radius of about two feet – because it had already been through the security clearance. We ended up propping it up on the counter because it was too big to go anywhere else, and its presence, although undoubtedly welcome, was certainly neither subtle nor elegant.

The security was tight beyond description and there were no chances taken. We had to construct the altar with lead inside it to make it bulletproof so that if a shot rang out, we could push the pope behind it for protection. The altar, without the lead, is now in the chapel of the diocesan pastoral center.

We made vestments for John Paul II, and although he didn't wear many of the vestments offered him in other places, he did in Phoenix. We were worried initially that we would have to make them capable of fitting over body armor, but thankfully that wasn't a problem.

The papal throne also had to be constructed with lead reinforcement and be bulletproof. There had to be a trapdoor on the stage area that ensured there was a place for the pope to escape from in case of attack. One of my fondest memories is that about two hours before the ceremony Archbishop Marini, who was then Monsignor Marini and the papal master of ceremonies, came to me and said, "Stay right with me and don't move."

As you can imagine, I was in a flurry of preparation because I was the local master of ceremonies, but this was the papal master of ceremonies giving me an order, so I complied without question. We went over the final arrangements of who was in this chair, and this chair, and this chair, and I kept replying "the Secret Service." Msgr. Marini finally said, "No, they can't be."

I said, "But they said this is where they said they want to be."

The Secret Service agent standing nearby overheard our conversation and came over and said, "We've been through this in every city, and we want to sit close by."

Marini answered, "Secret Service. So be a secret." And he moved the chairs off to the side of the stage under a palm tree, where they and the Secret Service remained.

We had asked the great humorist and writer Erma Bombeck to introduce the bishop and the Holy Father, which she graciously agreed to do. So when the Pope Mobile arrived at the stadium with John Paul II inside, Erma Bombeck was standing up in front of 80,000 telling Catholic jokes as only she could.

It was a wonderful experience meeting Erma and forming a friendship with her. She was a person of great faith, and her own brand of wisdom. Some years later, I was honored to be at her funeral mass, and we were reminded that her participation in the papal mass was one of the highlights of her life.

I remember that when we went to the first planning meeting in 1985, Msgr. Marini was not yet the papal master of ceremonies. The person who preceded him told us, "When the pope comes to your cities, everybody is going to want to drag him to every dog and pony show. But that is not why the pope is coming. He is coming to celebrate the eucharist with his people."

He also said, "If anyone of you is lucky enough to serve as the local master of ceremonies, you will discover as you kneel behind the pope that when he consecrates that bread and when he lifts that cup, it is a truly mystical experience for him, and will be for you, too."

I will attest to that. I did kneel five feet behind the Holy Father because I was blessed to be the local master of ceremonies. And kneeling there, despite the presence of all those bishops and cardinals, despite the presence of the crowd, the intensity of John Paul II as he celebrated the eucharist was overwhelming, and the experience amazed me. In fact, the entire mass was amazing in every aspect.

During the planning, we had to make certain that everything we did would set an appropriate precedent, because this was no ordinary celebration – it was a papal mass. The day of the mass was also the Feast of the Triumph of the Cross, and we included the anointing of the sick as part of the celebration.

I remember that morning standing on that field as a camera was installed on the cross, and I was debating (with a few curse words) with Marge Injasoulian about where the camera should be located. Lo and behold, she got her way, and the best pictures of the day came from the camera on the cross, placed where she had insisted it be placed.

So the memories of that time are plentiful, and they are vivid. To see the Holy Father celebrate mass, to see him with his people and his people with him, was simply incredible and absolutely unforgettable.

As far as I know, Phoenix was the first city to end a papal liturgy with a fireworks display. We set off more than $10,000 worth of fireworks in a couple of minutes, and it was spectacular to say the least. Of course the Secret Service was very nervous about the display because it would have been difficult to distinguish gunshots from fireworks, so we kept our plans secret from everybody but the Secret Service. So at the end of the mass, the fireworks went up, 80,000 people cheered, and the fireworks expressed for everybody what the experience of being with the pope was like.

The other intimate contact I had with him was in Rome in 1995. A group of us took about 100 teenagers from St. Timothy's in Mesa and about 40 teenagers from a parish in Georgia to go on a pilgrimage.

I called Archbishop Paul Marcinkus, former president of the Vatican Bank and a very influential force in the Vatican, and asked him for help in getting in to see the Holy Father while we were there. He made some calls, and told me who to ask for when we arrived in Rome.

When we got there, I called the brother that I had been referred to and he said, "Oh father, I'm very sorry, but the Holy Father isn't seeing pilgrims out at the summer residence, but I have tickets for you for the general audience on Wednesday."

I was a little disappointed, but still grateful that the kids would get to see John Paul II at the general audience. I remember that they sent the tickets and there were tickets for all the kids, and three that said "prima filia", which is Italian for "in front." At the time I didn't know precisely what it meant.

The national spokesperson for Life Teen, singer Kathy Troccoli, was with us, and we picked a teen by lot — Robert Sandoval — and the three of us took the prima filia tickets. We walked in holding those tickets, the Swiss Guard saluted, and we made our way towards the front row. We were a little late, and as we proceeded

I thought, "Oh, the kids are going to be so far in the back, but at least they will get to see the pope even if it's at a distance."

It turned out they had blocked off rows of seats on the other side of the aisle for Life Teen, so the kids were seated right up front. They were cheering and clapping, and a man with a camera approached me and said, "Father, what hotel are you staying at?"

I thought, "Oh, that's right, the pope will come in right up this aisle. So this man wants to take pictures and get them to me later."

I said something to him about the pope arriving near where we were sitting, and he answered me in broken English. "Pope no come here. You go there."

That's how I found out we were going to receive a blessing from the Holy Father.

At the end of the wonderful celebration, we went up on the stage and were presented to the Holy Father to receive his blessing for Life Teen. We went back down into our seats, and one of the officials came up to us and pointed and said "This way."

I asked myself, "Okay, what did I do wrong?"

But nothing was wrong. Indeed, we were taken back onto the stage, and then all the Life Teen kids were asked to come up for a photo with the Holy Father.

During the ceremony, people sang and celebrated in costume, and everything was very festive. But even in 1995, the pope was ailing. He held his hand up over part of his face, and was clearly very tired and not well.

But despite his evident weakness, he walked across the stage to the Life Teen kids, handed off his cane to one of his assistants, and started "high fiving" the kids. It was such a beautiful symbol for me to see how they filled him with life, and how energized he became by them. There are pictures of him reaching out to touch their faces, and just experience them.

There I was, standing there like a goofball, and having done one too many weddings, I put my hand around the pope and smiled for the camera. He started talking to me, and I thought of all the things I should say to the pope now that I had the chance. But he was asking me questions like how are you? How's your trip? Where are you going from here?

Then he said, "I remember the music and the liturgy in Phoenix."

I was stunned, and then I sinned. I said, "Thank you, Holy Father. I coordinated that mass."

I don't know why I said it. It was very prideful, but I was so surprised that the pope would remember the events of years before in Phoenix that the words just slipped out.

The next day, the teens all went to Florence and I stayed behind to go see Mother Teresa's sisters. As I walked through the Vatican and near the shops, I saw a wonderful picture of the pope on display. I went inside a little shop, and the proprietor said, "Gruppo, gruppo."

I asked, "Group?"

He reached for a copy of the Vatican newspaper, Observatory Romano, and there on the front page was that picture of the Life Teen members with the pope. This little shop happened to be the Observatory Romano's outlet store, and it also had for sale a videotape of the pope's session with us which I was able to purchase. The man had recognized me from the group.

There is no question that my life, young people's lives, and the life of anybody who went to a World Youth Day or any other event where the pope was present were impacted by Pope John Paul. In Rome, there were almost two million teenagers present, and I am sure some destinies were changed.

Life Teen had just a little taste of that. We did a eucharistic adoration, and Cardinal George from Chicago came and spoke to Life Teen on the Spanish steps. We brought out the eucharist, and like a wave the teens fell to their knees in the presence of the eucharist and there was absolute silence. There were thousands of teenagers there on the Spanish steps, but it is also a place where people gather.

The influence — both direct and indirect — that John Paul II had on people's prayer was immense.

After watching the broadcast of the pope's funeral, I went to Rome to be present when the new pope was elected. One of the precious gifts of that journey was to visit the place where John Paul was laid to rest. His body was already buried, but even at that point a couple of weeks after his death, people waited in line by the thousands to file by his burial place to pay their respects.

I also was able to spend time in prayer with the body of John XXIII, one of the two people who John Paul took his name from. John XXIII is up for canonization, and when he was beatified, his body was moved from the tomb where John Paul is now buried. John's body has not corrupted in 40 years, and is now on display in a glass case in the Vatican. Once again the line of people filing past was constant and numbered in the thousands. He is also a pope who is still loved by his people.

What was so beautiful to me at the funeral mass of John Paul was when the people started chanting, "Santo, santo, santo" – which meant "call him a saint." And of course Pope Benedict responded and has started the beatification process, and has waived the usual waiting period.

I was also moved by the signs that were hung up around the Vatican. They had a photo of the pope, and said, "Grazie, Papa."

The gratitude of the people of Rome and of the people of the world leaves little doubt that John Paul will be declared a saint. I also predict that he will be awarded some sort of prize, perhaps even the Nobel Peace Prize, posthumously. It would be strange if this didn't happen considering the influence he had on world politics and world issues.

His presence will linger for generations. His theology of the body of Christ is so deep, that once you read about it, it changes the entire way you look at humanity. The impact that John Paul had will be felt for hundreds of years, both in terms of his theology and on the impact his presence had.

CHAPTER 3
MOTHER TERESA OF CALCUTTA

There are probably not two more magical words in the world to evoke a positive response than "Mother Teresa." She belonged to everybody. It didn't matter what religion you were, or what kind of person you were. She just evoked positive feelings and love.

I always tell people that no matter what you have ever heard about, when you spent time with Mother Teresa it went beyond all the stories. You spent time with her, and you just teared up. Somebody would ask, "What are you crying about?" and the answer was, "I don't know."

She just spoke and emitted love in such a way that you couldn't not experience it. You could touch it, you could feel it, and you could smell it. At the same time, because she was so tiny and so wrinkled, she seemed as human as she was holy.

My relationship with her was one of the truly great gifts of my life.

It all started when a friend of mine named Merle Parker became a co-worker of Mother Teresa. She told me that Mother Teresa was going to San Francisco, and I should go up to see her. We had just started to do a television program on EWTN with Mother Angelica for Life Teen, and I thought it would be a great coup to get an interview with Mother Teresa.

I called the superior in San Francisco, whose name was Sister Sylvia. I told her who I was, and said, "Sister, I am begging you. I just need five minutes. I will come with cameras, and we just need a few moments with Mother Teresa for the teenagers in the United States."

Sister Sylvia said, "I'm sorry, father, but Mother Teresa doesn't like to do interviews. But if you come to San Francisco, you can spend the day with her and you can follow her around with the camera."

I thought it was amazing, and we got our team together — Fr. Jack Spaulding, Phil Baniewicz, Tom Booth, our cameraman — and we asked a great friend of ours in the media, Mary Jo West, to come with us.

I called Sister Sylvia about a week ahead of time to remind her that she had made a promise of spending time with Mother Teresa, and she said, "Oh yes, father, I remember. It's too bad you don't have an airplane."

I said, "What do you mean?"

She said, "Mother has to leave and fly to Gallup, and you could fly with her."

I said, "I'll call you back."

I called the head of America West Airlines. He got back and said, "I would love to, but we don't have any planes small enough that would land in Gallup."

So I called Charles Keating, who was a philanthropist - albeit a controversial one, but I knew him and his family – and I said, "Can I borrow an airplane to fly with Mother Teresa."

He graciously said yes.

So what happened is we flew up to San Francisco on Charles Keating's airplane and spent the day with Mother Teresa, and then got on the airplane and flew with Mother to Gallup from San Francisco.

Sitting on that airplane with her was amazing. She was already getting old and tired, but at any given time she would pull out her rosary and pray. There was food on the plane, but the sisters typically ate by themselves. They usually eat the leftovers from the poor.

I remember there were some bags of cookies from Pepperidge Farm. I remember Mother Teresa taking the bag and giving each of the sisters a cookie, almost like communion. Not that it was communion, but there was that much respect in her actions for each human being.

And then we sat at her feet and did an interview. I remembered sitting there, and I encountered the ugliest feet I have ever seen. As tiny as she was, her feet were as wide as they were long. The skin was cracked from her wearing sandals for a lifetime, and they showed all the signs of wear and hard work. I immediately thought of the scripture verse, "How beautiful are the feet of the ones who bring glad tidings."

We interviewed her – Fr. Jack Spaulding and me – and we asked her what she wanted to say to teenagers in the United States. I thought

I knew what she was going to say. I waited for her reply, "Tell them not to be so worldly, tell them not to be so commercial."

Instead, she looked at us and said, "Bring the young people to Jesus."

I said, "No, Mother, what would you like to say to the young people?"

I wanted her to say something about serving the poor or something like that, but she just patiently and lovingly repeated, "Bring the young people to Jesus."

Mary Jo West was talking to Mother Teresa and told her of her desire to adopt a child. Mother Teresa normally never allowed people to adopt children and bring them to foreign countries, but for some reason she looked at Mary Jo and said, "I will give you a child."

Ultimately she did, a beautiful baby named Mollie.

Tom Booth wrote Mother Teresa a song because he knew that she loved the Prayer of

Abandonment. He sang it for her, and she said, "Very beautiful, Tom. But you missed a line. Add a line here."

She corrected him. She was incredible, and nothing got past her.

When we arrived in Gallup, and saw how the people flocked to her, we asked her to come to Phoenix. She said, "I will come if the bishop asks me."

So the Keating family flew up in their other airplane and met with Mother in Gallup, and we set up a call for the Bishop of Phoenix to make to Mother Teresa, and he asked her to come. I got a beautiful letter back from Mother saying yes, she would send her sisters here.

Where we had two years to prepare for the arrival of Pope John Paul II, we had five days to prepare for the arrival of Mother Teresa.

I had to call the people who handled the rental of the Coliseum over the weekend at their homes. I had to get hold of the police department, who said, "But Father, she's not a head of state like the pope was. We can't provide any kind of security for her."

I said, "Well, I don't know that Mother needs any kind of security, but the people who show up to see her are certainly going to need it."

I turns out that we went from having no officers, to having 24 officers around the clock. We set up the event at the Veterans' Memorial Coliseum. We were worried that nobody would show up on such short notice, and we had 15,000 seats to fill.

Not only was it packed, but people were lined up around the building and were banging on the doors to get in. We had to lock the doors. We had asked for food donations for the poor in lieu of any kind of ticket fees, and there was so much food it was piled high.

Even people who couldn't get into the parking lot stacked up their food along 19th Avenue and McDowell. There were mountains of food, and people just driving by continued to add to it.

Mother's arrival in Phoenix sparked an intense response from almost everybody.

We had rented a little house for the sisters to start out in, and Phil Baniewicz (who was still a young man at the time) served as their driver because, of course, none of them drove. We had acquired a van – not a new one because we didn't think Mother Teresa would approve of that – but we did find one that was appropriate.

At one point as Phil drove along the road, Mother Teresa looked at him and said, "Phil, that's a beautiful cross you have. May I see it?"

So he took it from around his neck, and gave it to her. She looked at it closely and said, "Very beautiful. Where's Mary?"

So she took a medal out of her pocket, kissed it, and added a medal to the chain so he would have both the crucifix and the medal of the Blessed Mother.

When Mother Teresa talked to you, there was nobody else in the world. You were the most important concern she had at that exact moment. You were it. This was perhaps her most striking characteristic, and what I remember the most clearly about her.

We had an event at Ss. Simon and Jude Cathedral, and Mother said, "I've never seen people react the way they reacted in Phoenix."

She was referring to the media coverage, and all the attention. She said that whenever somebody took a picture of her, she always asked Jesus to take somebody from purgatory and let them into heaven because it was such a penance for her. She really did not enjoy the camera.

There was a woman who grabbed Mother Teresa by the arm, which was a little frightening because Mother was so tiny. She was wailing and squeezing her arm as she said, "Please pray for my son. He's dying of AIDS. Please pray for my son."

Mother told the woman she would pray for her son, and I pried the woman's fingers as gently as I could off of Mother's arm. I said, "Mother told you she would pray, and she will."

We swooped into the van, and headed off to our next stop.

The next day when Phil was driving, Mother said suddenly, "Phil, pull over."

Phil said, "Mother, we have a police escort. I can't just pull over."

She repeated, "Pull over."

So, Phil pulled over. There was a man standing alone at the side of the road. She went up to him, and we weren't sure what was said. She handed him a medal, and got back in the van.

Later, the other sisters told us that the man was the son of the woman who had stopped her the night before. When Mother went up to him, he asked for prayers because he was dying of AIDS. She had answered him, "I know. I talked to your mother."

When people hear that story, their minds have a hard time grasping it. But when you live in the spirit as Mother Teresa did, nothing was far-fetched.

One of the most treasured moments I had with Mother Teresa was when she said to me, "I'd like to speak to your governor."

I said, "Okay," even though I didn't know Governor Rose Mofford at the time. I picked up the phone and managed to get through to the governor's secretary, who as luck would have it knew me from the parish. I said, "I am here with Mother Teresa, who would like to speak to Governor Mofford."

The secretary said, "The governor is in a meeting, but let me get a message to her and I will get back with you right away."

In the meantime, Mother Teresa was having a conversation with some people, and the phone rang. It was Governor Mofford, who asked to speak to Mother Teresa.

I said, "Mother, Governor Mofford is on the phone for you."

And that little lady ran to the phone. She literally flew across the room. She got on the phone and asked Governor Mofford to come to the prayer group that night, and the governor said yes, she would come. So I had the unique privilege of introducing our governor, who is still a very tall and incredibly loving lady, to this very short and incredibly loving lady.

And the two hit it off and were instant friends, even though they couldn't have been any different. Rose Mofford had piles of white hair stacked up on her head, and you couldn't even see Mother's hair because it was tucked away. Rose was tall, Mother Teresa was short. But their hearts as people were the same.

They had a wonderful visit together, and then this shrewd little lady went out and said to the 15,000 people that had gathered to see her, "I'm so glad that the governor is here, and I would like to ask the governor for a home for the poor people."

Every television station in the state of Arizona was there along with the 15,000 people, and Rose Mofford got up and said, "Mother, I will give you that home."

Afterwards, the governor grabbed me and said, "And you are going to help me build it."

That is when my friendship began with Rose Mofford, who was and remains one of the great, great people in the state of Arizona. It is a relationship that has gone deep and long, and it started that night at that moment.

We built the home for Mother Teresa, and what a joy it was to do. Unlike any other project I've ever been involved with, people couldn't do enough to help me. I'd ask them for something, and there was no hesitation. The yes came immediately to whatever I requested. I'd call a potential source of help and say, "You know, I'm trying to get this home built for Mother Teresa…" and whoever it was I had on the phone wouldn't even let me finish the request. I'd hear, "Whatever it is you need, it's yours."

One of my favorite stories about Mother Teresa is tied to her habit of traveling with no money. She didn't carry a penny. One of her first days in Phoenix, she said to me, "Father, people have been giving me money to help the sisters get started here in Phoenix. Would you mind putting it in the bank for us so they can begin to serve the poor?"

I said, "Certainly, Mother. I will be happy to."

So she started unloading the pockets of her gray sweater, and I just transferred everything into my own pockets. After I got home that night, I began to unravel what I had to put it into order so I could go to the bank for her the next day. I found I had $33,000 that people had just given to her.

Before Mother left Phoenix, we drove her around Phoenix and she saw the homeless lying around in the parks and on the streets. She said, "This is the kind of poverty you don't see in lots of places."

This was reported in the newspaper, and there were people who took offense at her words or who made fun of what she said. Their sarcasm ran to remarks like, "Oh yes, our poverty here is so much worse than Calcutta's."

What she was saying is that in most places you don't see people alone. In other places there is great poverty, but the poor have each other. There is community, and the poverty does not always carry the stigma that it does in this country.

Here what she saw are single people totally alone. The greatest poverty in her eyes was spiritual poverty, not just physical.

When Mother left Phoenix, four sisters remained to serve, and they have continued to serve all these years.

I also had the tremendous experience of being with Mother Teresa when Life Teen was doing a television show in Guadalupe, Mexico. We ran into Mother Teresa, and went to see her sisters there. Phil

Baniewicz and I also went to Tijuana to see Mother Teresa when she had her heart attack and was recovering.

I went to New York for the celebration of the sisters being in the United States. I will never forget the experience of being at St. Patrick's Cathedral. My friend singer Kathy Troccoli came with us, and the kindness of Cardinal Law is forever in my memory. I don't know what other people say – I just know how he was with me.

The memories I have of Mother Teresa are precious to me, and I think about her and her life every day. Before she left, she gave me a rosary and I had it in a case. A friend of mine who is very spiritual was here from New York, and she stood and looked at the rosary for a long time. She finally said, "May I just hold it?"

I said, "Of course."

She started to weep just holding Mother Teresa's rosary, and I knew what I had to do. I said, "It's yours. Please take it."

My friend said, "No, I couldn't possibly take it."

I told her, "I have it sitting in this case. And you're going to pray it."

I knew that I couldn't just leave it in the case. Mother Teresa would want me to give the rosary away.

My friend, whose name is Breda, tells me stories about who has borrowed the rosary to pray. One of the most comforting things to me – and I know it sounds pious and spiritual – is to hear "you have a friend in heaven." But I truly believe that we do have a friend in heaven in the form of Mother Teresa.

I believe strongly that when we look back on history, we will regard John Paul II as one of the great figures of the 20th century. But I also think that Mother Teresa will be the St. Francis of the 20th century. Her impact on the world as a whole was tremendous, and continues to this day. And much like John Paul II's appeal went beyond religious boundaries and social boundaries, so did hers.

The fact that she won a Nobel Peace Prize is certainly significant, but truly none of that meant anything to her.

People talk now about how Mother Teresa struggled with bouts of depression. Some respond to this revelation by saying, "See, she wasn't such a saint after all."

But speaking as somebody who has had bouts of depression himself, I can only say that the fact that she served the way she did despite being depressed proves even more how wonderful she was.

It is one thing to be a figure of power or of great holiness and command attention. But it's quite another to be a little tiny woman under five feet tall, who could walk into the office of a president or a ruler in any country and get somebody to listen to her. She could attract media and crowd attention anywhere anytime, and she could have gathered an immense amount of earthly power if she had chosen to do so. And she did not.

She was focused on individuals and their individual needs, and what God wanted her to do to help them all. She certainly loved priests, and during really difficult times in my life since her death I have taken comfort in the firm knowledge that Mother Teresa is in heaven praying for me.

My life went a direction I never expected. But I know that the love I experienced from Mother was VERY real, and I know that no matter what, I hope to imitate Mother's love for others.

CHAPTER 4
LEARNING TO LIVE WITH DEATH

When I was growing up, death was not a big part of my life. I don't remember anybody close to me dying. I do remember driving by mortuaries and thinking what really weird, frightening places they were. I never really got the connection when I started thinking about entering the priesthood about being a priest and having to deal with death.

After I was entered the seminary, a couple of things happened. My grandmother died, and I flew back to Cleveland to be with the family. I remember some of my Polish relatives wanting me to take a picture standing next to the casket. I thought that it was unusual and very odd, but they seemed quite comfortable around Grandma's body. I really wasn't.

I remember also seeing a movie that contained a scene of a priest leaning up against a body and leading a rosary. I thought, "There is no way I could ever do that. There is no way on earth that I am ever going to be able to lean up against a body and lead people in prayer."

I was absolutely certain that a body was going to wink at me. I was sure one was going to move. I have no idea now what I was so fearful of back then.

In the seminary, I had to take a tour of a mortuary. I was literally freaked being required to see a body and how it was embalmed, and in being made to go into a casket room. I tried to be calm, but inside I think I was almost screaming.

A short time after becoming a priest, and just a few days after starting at St. Jerome, I got called out to visit a sick man in the middle of the night.

When I went to the home, I found an elderly man on a couch with his family positioned all around him. It was clear that he was dying.

Because it was my first anointing, I was very nervous. As I anointed him, he died in my arms. I think he was waiting for the priest to arrive to let go. He held on to receive his final blessing and forgiveness of the Catholic church, and then died with me holding his head.

I wish I could say that I experienced an epiphany and was transformed by the experience. I could say it, but it wouldn't be the truth. What I actually did do is go back to the rectory and take a shower because I felt like I was wearing death.

Fortunately, I met a nun named Sr. Teresa Marie McIntyre who was an expert on death and grief. I convinced the pastor, Fr. Richard Moyer, to hire her to work with the sick and the dying. Eventually, this nun blew me and my fears right out of the water.

We called her Sr. Death and Dying, partially to tease her and partially because she was a proponent of the stages of death that had first been suggested by Elizabeth Kubler Ross.

I remember Sr. Teresa Marie saying that when she died she wanted it to be from cancer because when she was born the first time, she didn't get to observe any of the birth. So if she was to be born a second time into eternal life, she didn't want to miss any piece of the journey.

She didn't want to get hit by a Greyhound bus and die. No quick exits without warning for this woman. She wanted to have things in place and experience her second birth.

Because of her outlook on dying as being a natural and universal part of life, I began to change how I faced death.

Through the years, I have had to bury babies, and theirs are still the hardest deaths for me to comprehend. I've buried teenagers who have died in accidents or as a result of cancer and other illnesses. I have buried people who have died at their own hands through suicide.

I remember being called to a home for a young man who died accidentally as a result of autocrotic asphyxiation, which is a sexual practice that involves a person hanging himself as he masturbates. When I was called that night I was at a point in my priesthood where nothing much shocked me anymore, and I was much more comfortable with death.

The victim's family wanted me to pray over his body. However, the young police officer who had been called to the scene would not let me go into the room. It was now a crime scene.

I said, "Please get your supervisor out here."

In fact, I had just married the chief of police for that city and I knew the supervisor on duty. When the supervisor did emerge, he said, "Oh Father Dale, please come right in."

After he left, the young officer said to me, "I'm sorry, Father, I wasn't trying to be tough. I was just having such a hard time dealing with what I saw that I didn't want you to see it."

His intent was to save me from being upset by the experience of witnessing the manner in which the young man had died. He was protecting and serving, trying to do his job just as I was. I thanked him for his concern, and told him I would be okay. And I prayed over the body without flinching.

I have seen people who shot themselves, whose blood went from floor to ceiling. Those situations are never easy to face, but one of the worst cases I ever dealt with was the death of a woman who had killed herself by drinking insecticide.

The body was in a terrible state, and the smell was hideous. I had to find the words to tell the family how she died. There are only so many ways without getting too graphic to let grieving relatives understand that there is no way there is going to be a viewing at the funeral home.

Even though dealing with death is never a matter of routine, I have become much more familiar with it and I know what dying with dignity really is.

I had a very close friend named Rose Totino. Most people recognize her name because of Totino's Party Pizza, which is something that always tickled her. However, her successes just began with pizza. She was the first female vice president of Pillsbury, and had come up with the formula to freeze pizza that she eventually sold to Pillsbury.

She was a little Italian woman, and I thought she was an amazing personality. She was a true benefactor of Life Teen. She donated thousands of dollars to Life Teen and its work, bought camera equipment, and was generous in every possible way.

One night she visited a Life Teen meeting and chatted with the teens. One of them asked her, "Why do you give so much money away?"

Rose answered, "Because I've never seen a hearse with a U-Haul hitched to the back of it."

She eventually had a stroke and became very ill, and was a patient at Mayo Clinic in Minnesota. Her daughters, Joanne and Bonnie, were very gracious and allowed me to come spend a day with them. Rose was paralyzed on one side, but her mind was still sharp. The hours I spent with her were precious ones, and the time was pure gold.

At the end of the day when I got ready to leave to fly back to Phoenix, Rose and I were alone in the room. I asked her, "Rose, what are you feeling?"

She said, "Father Dale, I'm happy."

I said, "You know, there's nothing to be afraid of."

She said, "I'm not afraid. He bids his angels to watch over me."

I replied, "When Jesus comes, it's going to be beautiful."

By this time, I was crying like a baby because I knew we were saying goodbye. She looked at me, and quoted scripture. "Eye has not seen nor ear has heard the glory that is revealed to those who love Him."

I said, "Thank you, Rose, for everything – for what you have done for me, for Life Teen, and for so many people."

And she said, "You know, I promised you $80,000 to start the fund to build the Life Teen studios."

I said, "I know, but you don't worry about that."

She said, "I just want you to know it's all taken care of."

I said, "Rose, that's not my concern."

And she replied, "Well, it might not be yours, but it's mine. I keep my promises to God. It's all taken care of."

Then this little Italian lady put her finger right up to my face and shook it and said, "You build that studio, and then you tell those young people that God loves them. You tell the hardest ones to reach that God loves them."

I was weeping, I told her I loved her, and I left. And then I got on the plane and went home to Phoenix.

I called Mayo's the next morning from Arizona to see how Rose was doing. Her daughters told me that when they walked into Rose's room that morning, they found their paralyzed mother sitting straight up with her hands stretched out.

She told them that she had seen the light. After that, she didn't speak again. She lay back down, and died a little while later.

Even in death, Rose Totino was the embodiment of immense dignity, hope, understanding, and comprehension of what this life is about. And what eternal life is about.

I returned to participate in the vigil service that was held at Totino Grace High School in Fridley, Minnesota. They had her body lying in state in the gymnasium, and there was literally a line of people around the gymnasium filing past her body. Almost to a person, everybody had a story about what Rose Totino had done to help them. College students, business people, and private citizens said things like, "I wrote to her and asked for help and she sent me money."

Throughout her life, charities had received millions and millions from Rose, all because she had understood that the day was going to come when she was going to see her maker. She was surrounded by love during her life, and by the time she died she had touched a lot of people.

Years after Rose died, I learned that one of my brother priests who lived with me – Fr. Marcel Salinas, who was a great man and a great priest – had stomach cancer.

Fr. Marcel belonged to a religious order, and typically when something like a terminal illness strikes a priest who belongs to an order, he returns to the mother house to be cared for. However, we decided together that he would stay at St. Tim's and die where he had lived. Bishop O'Brien came to see him and said, "This changes everything," meaning that Fr. Marcel would die among the people who loved him.

I had a dog at the time, a cocker spaniel, and Fr. Marcel and Lifer and didn't get along at all. As luck would have it, Lifer was getting old and sick at the same time that Fr. Marcel was dying. At one moment we were gathered around Marcel's room praying, and Lifer came into the room panting. Then he got up on the side of the bed.

At that moment, we weren't really sure whether Marcel was alive or dead. But suddenly his eyes opened, and this pious priest looked up and said, "Shit, I'm going to die before the damn dog does."

Suddenly, everything was put into perspective.

One of the great voices in contemporary music – both Christian and popular – belongs to my friend Kathy Troccoli. I will never forget Kathy calling Fr. Marcel on the phone and singing him one of his favorite songs, "My Life Is in Your Hands," as he was dying.

I will also never forget rolling him in his wheelchair into the church on a Thursday night. Fifteen hundred people had shown up to pray over him at his anointing. The love that flowed back and forth between Fr. Marcel and the ones gathered to support him was something so powerful we were all changed by it, and the evening was a once in a lifetime experience for all of us.

The deaths of so many people have transformed me and my understanding of the end of this life, which was certainly helpful during the time of my own father's death. Although he had been having some health problems, my dad died suddenly and without any real warning.

I happened to be driving to the chancery on the day my father was undergoing tests, when I decided to go to the hospital instead. My mom had called beforehand to tell me my father was going to have a couple of things checked out, but she said not to bother to come and that she would call me when everything was finished.

However, something came over me and I decided to drive straight to the hospital instead of going downtown. I just knew I had to go immediately. I arrived at the hospital, parked my car, and made my way back to the wing where my father was undergoing tests. As I was walking down the hall, I saw doctors and nurses talking to my mother, and my mother began to cry. My father had passed away one minute before I got there.

In going through my father's death and experiencing the impact it had on me, my mother and my family, I gained some knowledge that helped during the final days of another treasured friend and truly good man, Cotton Fitzsimmons. He was truly one of the great NBA coaches, but he was also one of the greatest people I have ever met.

In the last few days of Cotton's life, his wife Joanne, some close friends, and I formed a team with the hospice nurses to ensure that somebody was with Cotton 24 hours a day. Carol and Dwayne from Nike, Julie Fie from the Phoenix Suns' office, Kevin Johnson's mother, Georgia, and I all took turns keeping a vigil. I would come and go and sleep on their couch, and then return to the parish.

What I saw in Cotton Fitzsimmons was a man whose presence affected so many people – both famous and ordinary – because he had a way of making everybody feel important. Whether you were a clerk at a Bashas' grocery store or a world famous figure, you were an important person as far as he was concerned. He treated everybody the same, which was with great kindness and respect. To see that he died with the same dignity that he had given to everybody else throughout his life was a phenomenal gift.

As I watched Pope John Paul II die, I once again experienced his incredible dignity. Because he died before the world as he let the world see him deteriorate, death was elevated to a whole new level. It became a universal experience to be shared.

Death has become one of the most expected aspects of my life. I have seen death in many ways, and have learned that each person has a unique way of coping with the issues surrounding loss.

Years ago when the father of my friend died, I went into the casket room at the mortuary with Greg. He threw off some quips like, "Do you have anything in a red two-door", and "Is there one with a stereo?" He handled his grief with humor.

I've seen people face death with anger, and rage at the doctors and nurses. I've also been present for a lot of death bed conversions where people got things off their chests. In a sense, they got rid of the baggage before they made the really big trip.

I have helped parents bury small children, or adult children, and witnessed their agony over losing their kids. It is hard to know what to say to parents who are grieving, so sometimes you just have to be there with them as they deal with their suffering. The fact is there sometimes aren't words to help. Sometimes all you can do is just be a source of comfort, and silence can be a part of that. But you have to be present.

I had the privilege of concelebrating mass for Erma Bombeck at her funeral. I have been present when people of stature and fame die — people who belong to everybody – and they experience death as we all do eventually. Some of their families were left in intense, relentless pain.

However, I have come to realize that for the person dying, death is not something to be feared. It's nothing to be rushed into, and I'm not suggesting that. But I have come to know it as another birth, with many of the same characteristics, including emerging into the unknown. I do believe that regardless of what else heaven may hold, it is filled with friends and family I have loved, who I hope continue to pray for me as they always did.

Death is about surrender. If you believe, then you handle it with grace and dignity.

Sister Teresa Marie McIntyre — Sister Death and Dying — went on a retreat with a group of teenagers, and my staff members and me. She had us each take 15 little pieces of paper. On the first five, we each had to write down five people who were important to us, and then on another five we wrote down material possessions that were most important, then five creature comforts (things we enjoyed like eating Big Macs, watching television, taking a bubble bath, playing baseball, whatever it was). We took the teens on an imaginary journey, and at each point they had to rip up one piece of paper from each category.

We never took them to the point where they had to eliminate everything, because we were afraid that some of the teens were so sensitive that if they got to the point where they had to rip up the paper representing mom or dad, it would just be too much and too traumatic. But we wanted to show them that death is really the final letting go of the things of this world.

What we wanted them to realize is that people who have something to cling to in the next world handle the letting go of the things in this world completely differently.

I encounter death very differently these days. I am not afraid to be with somebody as death approaches. It is a sacred time, and its hours are filled with experiences to be treasured.

I am no longer afraid of dead bodies. I would never want to be a mortician, and I have great respect and gratitude for the folks who provide those services.

I am no longer afraid of my own death. I know I have friends on the other side, and I know that dying will be an awesome journey. I'd prefer that my own departure time not be any time too soon, but I am no longer frightened at the thought of it.

What Rose Totino told me is true: "Eye has not seen nor ear has heard the glory that will be revealed to those that love Him."

Letting go of things in this life – people, titles, and possessions – are all mini-deaths. They teach us how to let go and trust God when our major-death occurs.

CHAPTER 5
PRIESTS – CAIN AND ABEL
WERE BROTHERS, TOO

One of the reasons I wanted to write this book was to reveal the humanity of priests. Truly, God uses the weak to confound the strong.

Priests are just human beings. It is one thing to say that, but it is another matter entirely to really come to understand what that means.

Priests are just people. They have likes and dislikes, preferences and prejudices. Some like sports, and some don't. Some like to drink, some don't. Some like to drink too much and, as we know, alcoholism has long been a problem in the priesthood.

Some like to go to the movies, and some like to vacation. Some like to play cards, and some like to play golf. They are human beings with all the variations and differences that any other group of people share.

Some priests know how to dress well, and some don't. Some keep things clean and neat, and some are messy people. Some are converts, some are cradle Catholics. Some come from loving families, and some come from dysfunctional families.

Priests come from all different background and cultures. There is always a variety of reasons why a man becomes a priest. Maybe a parent was pushing. Maybe it was an escape. Maybe it truly was an inner call from the Lord.

The truth of the matter is, just as there are good doctors and not-so-good doctors, there are good priests and not-so-good priests. There are priests who are givers, and there are takers.

I really want to talk about how priests treat one another, because it's not something that most people see. And when they do, they are often shocked. I have no desire to put down brother priests, but wish only to give insight into how the priesthood is lived in America.

In marriage, you have instant accountability. If you are crabby or selfish, there's somebody (and usually several somebodies) – a spouse, your children, your parents, your in-laws – to give you immediate feedback. Granted, that system isn't perfect in marriage, either. There's a lot of wedlock that's deadlocked out there. But at least there is a system of checks and balances in place, even if it's sometimes flawed.

In a good marriage, you build a rapport that permits you to tell the other person when he or she has really stepped in it, so to speak. You can say, "I don't think you're being fair," or "I don't think you're seeing this right." When there's love, maturity has a chance to flourish and a person grows in wisdom as part of a couple.

Priests don't have that.

You have little accountability for the things that really matter in life. It's not that you don't get feedback from parishioners, but very often it's just surface stuff that provokes little if any discussion at all. You just write it off. There are plenty of other people around to tell you how wonderful you are.

That lack of accountability becomes a serious problem for priests, and that lack of healthy accountability can actually be tragic. Whatever weaknesses we have in life, they either get worse as we get older, or we have to begin to conquer those demons – lack of patience, anger, alcoholism. If these kinds of weaknesses plague a marriage, they end up damaging or destroying a relationship and a tearing apart a family. If they plague a priest, he can disintegrate right along with his calling.

Weaknesses begin to emerge in priests as time goes on. Addictions, anger issues – they all begin to come out because life gets more and more stressful, unless you're really lucky. Not too many priests have anybody in their lives to tell them that they're getting off track until they're really in trouble.

There are in the priesthood some absolutely wonderful human beings who are loyal, loving, and genuinely supportive of each other. And there are some individuals wearing priestly vestments who are extremely unhappy and unhealthy, and destructive.

If you ask where the dysfunction of priests comes from, I am sure celibacy is part of the issue. It probably comes from our families of origin, too. Does it come from seminary life? I'm sure that's also part of it.

Does it come from a lifestyle that is emotionally selfish? I am certain that is also a factor.

It's an unreal lifestyle not to have to share the television remote with somebody. It's an unreal lifestyle to always have what you want for dinner every night. It's an unreal lifestyle to never have to ask somebody else about spending money. Those basic things truly can create a selfish person, even if that person doesn't intend to become self-centered. However, it's very easy to become the center of your own universe.

To focus in on seminary life, there's no question it's not a normal life. It's not supposed to be. The seminary exists to train men to enter lives that are going to be radically different than those being lived by most other people.

I always found it interesting that the church spends so much time and energy talking people into becoming priests because there is such a shortage, and then spends the next eight years of a man's life telling him what's wrong with him. In the seminary, you do get feedback. You get it from other seminarians with whom you live and work, you get it in the classroom from the faculty. There is so much feedback, in fact, that some people just start to turn it off. They don't hear it any more.

But when you leave the seminary, all of that feedback stops. It just doesn't exist any longer, unless you become a member of some kind of priest support group.

Many people don't understand exactly what a priest support group is supposed to be. In general, it is usually a group of three to six priests who share a bond, come together to pray, and who have a very honest relationship with each other. They support each other, but what is at the foundation of that fundamental support is truth.

The priests in your support group are the ones (or should be the ones) who will be the most honest with you. There were guys who came and went in my group, but over the years there remained a steady core. Fr. Chuck Kieffer and Fr. Mike Straley and I were there for each other for a long time. During both the good times and the bad times in my life (and there has been an abundance of each), they were constant sources of insight and encouragement for me. They were there, regardless.

In the priesthood, there are basically three classifications of people. Group one is your support group and the priests you are most friendly with. For me, that was Fr. Jack Spaulding, Msgr. Richard Moyer, Fr. Mark Dippre, and Bishop Thomas O'Brien — friends of that depth and caliber. These were the men who — although they may or may not be your official support group — are the ones who stand by you and who both raise you up or hold you down, depending on what you need at any given time.

The second group consists of men who are genuinely kind and positive human beings who want to help each other and who view the priesthood as a brotherhood. They want to give of themselves not only in prayer, but also emotionally and financially. They will be there for brother priests however it is in their power to help.

Then there is a third group. These priests are angry, jealous, and gossipy. They are spiritually bored, and are very often burned out with ministry. They can be hostile towards each other, and they are ambitious in a negative way. They really can be threatened by the success of others, and often do what they can do to hold back those who would move forward.

I have had many people say to me "The Catholic church in the United States needs another Bishop Fulton Sheen." It really does. The church desperately needs somebody who can preach to the general public, who can reach out and capture their hearts and imagination with the sheer force of personality, and make it possible for everybody – not just Catholics – to see the power of faith.

People need to know a faith that isn't angry, or yelling, or any of the kinds of things that drive people from the pews in droves. People need faith like the faith that Bishop Sheen gave the Catholic church.

Unfortunately, it's not going to happen. Priests won't let it happen.

Priests tear down somebody who starts being lifted up in that way. It's not just priests, either. Certain lay persons enjoy pulling down priests, too. They diminish a priest by saying things like, "He's too flashy, he's too conservative, he's too liberal, I don't like the way he does mass, I don't approve of the car he drives."

Even when a priest becomes a bishop, he begins his ministry in controversy. It's pure office politics. The buzz starts immediately: He has his "in" group, he has his cronies, he wants to be an archbishop, he's going to do this, he's going to do that, etc. There is no difference between what a new bishop faces, and what any CEO of any big company has to endure when he's new on the job. The group around the figurative water cooler can be treacherous.

Rumors about priests are deadly. They circulate among the priests, and among the people in and out of the pews.

Several years ago I read an article that contained interviews with young men who had been asked about becoming priests. The expectation was that they would not want to enter the priesthood because of the requirement for celibacy. Yet what the interviewer discovered is that it was not celibacy that repelled young men from the priesthood, but the negativity.

The things their parents said about priests, the things that other people said about priests – these factors weighed heavily on their minds. They responded with remarks like, "Why would I want to enter a life where you're always in danger of being slandered yet you're not being compensated financially like you are if you're a celebrity and end up in the pages of the National Enquirer? You're not being paid with power, like a politician is paid. You can say whatever you want about an issue and it won't have any affect whatsoever because somebody else is still going to have more influence than you ever will."

Negativity, rumors, and disturbed priests really create chaos.

My seminary experience was a good one, even though it wasn't ideal. My training left me with expectations of more friendship and camaraderie. I thought there would be loyalty and brotherhood, but as a whole it does not exist. The basic ideals of any neighborhood Boy Scout troop don't find a home in the priesthood.

If you want to talk about "priest scandals" I think how priests treat each other is scandalous, and must be to God.

For many years, a priest in the parish next door to me was one who spread all kind of rumors. He tried to get people together who didn't like me, or who had negative things to say about me. He actually collaborated with the media to get negative publicity in circulation.

One time when I asked him if we could talk, he actually said to me, "No. I just got over my hatred of the bishop."

I was so stunned that a priest of God would use those words. He stated that he had hated the bishop. This is somebody who talked a lot about mercy when he preached.

The way I took his remark was that he had just gotten over his hatred of the bishop, so he wasn't ready to give up his hatred of me and have a conversation. I was both amazed and puzzled. How can you both serve and hate?

Those conflicts are part of the human condition; there is no doubt about it. And I believe we will continue to have discussions about whether priests should be celibate or not.

People frequently ask me if I think that married priests could solve the problems of the Catholic church. My stock answer to that question is that it doesn't matter what I think.

I once stated that on a radio program. "My opinion isn't important. I'm not the pope."

But I truly don't have any great insight about whether a married clergy would be a solution or just another problem. Like many other men, I would really have liked to be married. But I don't have any real knowledge of whether married clergy would help or hinder the priesthood, regardless of whether or not I would have been happier. And since my preferences are not the sum total of the Catholic church's tradition, they really aren't a pertinent part of any debate.

However, unless we work hard at ordaining and keeping priests who are happy and healthy, and in accountable relationships – unless we get priests who take the command of Jesus to love as their primary command, as it is to any Christian – the priesthood is in deep trouble.

The priesthood is not a boys' club. It's not a country club. It's not supposed to be an inner circle that keeps other people out. But unlike the apostles who were called to love and care for each other, the priesthood won't have credibility until its members are faithful to each other. It won't have the credibility that Jesus wants it to have in terms of saying to families, married couples and single folks, to warring nations, and to the world that love conquers.

In conclusion, I want to offer some thoughts about what has become known as the "priest scandal." I was in the middle of it, and I can also see it from the outside.

People want to know what scandal is doing to the average priest, and what it's doing to the priesthood. I think one thing it has done is give the priesthood a new dose of humility, which is a blessing.

I think it has given many priests, including me, a deeper understanding of mercy. Priests will be better confessors. They will be aware of how easy it is to fall, how easy it is to sin.

I think all of us who are or were in the priesthood are embarrassed by the scandal. I know myself that it can be embarrassing to put on a Roman collar. It's like pinning a target to your neck. I know that public scrutiny and cynicism are much higher than ever before. It's a witch hunt out there, and nobody is safe from it.

People are looking for reasons for priests to fall. I think that the scandal has deeply affected the psyche of our priests and ministers. It has also made men in the seminary, the young guys, much more conservative and much more aware that they don't want to burn themselves out in ministry. So they are holding back, and not fully embracing the call to serve. They are coming out of the seminary with many more boundaries, some of which are good and some of which are undoubtedly not so good.

The priest scandals in the United States have impacted every priest. The backlash makes priests suspect and distrust each other, and it has created great fear. If somebody wanted to set out to destroy the Catholic church, a good way to do it would be to destroy the priesthood. Much of the Catholic church depends on the ministry of priests.

I am not saying this to lower in any way the significance of what is done by lay people to serve, or to minimize the vocations of families and parents, and so forth. However, Catholics are so sacramentally dependent on priests for the eucharist, for anointing and reconciliation that if you want to bring down the Catholic church, just bring down the priests.

Having a disunified body has opened the priesthood for all kinds of issues. Negative groups are now free to drive a figurative Mack truck right over the presbyterate.

Because the original priesthood was created by Jesus, I believe it won't be destroyed. The way priests treat each other and the realization by the Catholic church's adversaries that it could be done in by doing in the priesthood – these two elements together have created a real challenge for Catholic evangelization in the United States.

Letting go of the Catholic priesthood was hard for me. It was my identity. But, once I could see there was no potential for me to LOVE – and no real love in the priesthood of Phoenix – I could move on. My conscience is clear!

Chapter 6
Cheer, Cheer for Old Notre Dame

I've learned during my life that one of the most important things is self-knowledge — learning to know who you are and who you aren't, and learning to accept yourself.

Acceptance has all kinds of levels. Liking how they look is very difficult for many people. Accepting what your gifts and limitations are — not that you shouldn't continue to strive to overcome obstacles — provides a very healthy approach to life. A great sense of peace comes about when you accept yourself.

For me as a child growing up, knowing that I had a big nose — which was literally always in front of my eyes — was something that drove me crazy until one day when I just got to the point that I said, "Okay, so I've got a big nose."

Part of self-knowledge was for me the acceptance that I am not a very gifted human being. I say this not as any form of false humility or put down, but as a simple statement of fact. I don't have a lot of innate gifts.

But, as I have told many people, I do know what my few gifts truly are. I can find the right person to do a job. I am also not afraid of failure. Any successes that I have had come from those two characteristics — the willingness to try, and the willingness to bring the right people in to help.

I can't sing, although I wish I could. I can't play music, although I wish I could. I am not an artist, although I love art. And I can't learn languages.

I once took a class with a tutor who had taught John F. Kennedy to speak Spanish. She told me that she had never dealt with anybody who spoke Spanish as badly as I did. I said, "Thank you very much."

That doesn't mean that I can't work at speaking Spanish or get better at it, but I don't have the gift of learning languages so the chances are I'm never going to be fluent.

One day I was at the parish. The bishop at the time, Bishop James Rausch — for whom I had a deep love — and the chancellor of the diocese, Fr. Jack Spaulding — who turned out to be one of my best friends — came to see me at the rectory. The bishop said that he would like me to go study liturgy and he would like me to do it in Rome.

I already had a great love of liturgy. In the seminary I was the liturgy coordinator, and I had continued to do a lot of reading and learning. I also had the great experience of getting involved with a company, North American Liturgy Resources, a music publishing company for liturgical music.

The bishop knew all these things, and when he asked me to go study in Rome I was very excited. However, I was dismayed when

I found out that the program I would be a part of required that I learn Italian.

I knew that it would be an incredible struggle for me. I didn't think I would master enough language to order a plate of spaghetti, much less study liturgy. So I got some information and returned to the bishop.

I told him that I wanted to study liturgy, but learning Italian would be such a problem for me that it would probably defeat the purpose of me going to Rome. I asked if I could go to Notre Dame instead because they had a program that would permit me to earn a masters in liturgy over four or five summers.

I also assured him that the program had a great reputation. Bishop Rausch said he would speak to some other bishops to make sure Notre Dame's program was right for me. He called back after a few days and said he approved the idea.

So I applied to the University of Notre Dame's program in liturgy in the spring of 1981, and was accepted. Shortly after that, we came up with the plan that I would go to school during the summers, and when I was not in school I would work at the chancery as the Vicar of Worship for the remaining nine months a year.

I received the letter appointing me to the position of Vicar of Worship and outlining this plan the day after Bishop Rausch died suddenly of a heart attack while standing in the line for the pharmacy at a grocery store. He had stopped in to purchase some antacids because he thought he had indigestion.

I remember I was at lunch with Monsignor Moyer because it was the anniversary of my priesthood. We got a page to go to the hospital because the bishop was sick, and he had been taken to a hospital very close to the parish where we both lived. By the time we responded, Bishop Rausch had been pronounced dead.

Thomas O'Brien was the Vicar General and was appointed to run the diocese, and he told me to just go ahead with the plans. So I prepared to head off to the University of Notre Dame for my first summer, which was really hard because I didn't know who the new bishop would be. Everything seemed like one giant unknown.

Although I was excited about going to graduate school, it was a new adventure. I also knew myself well enough to know that I am not the sharpest knife in the drawer. I am not the smartest person in any classroom, and I kept wondering how I was going to go to Notre Dame and complete an advanced program.

My best friend, Mark Keough, and I got into my white Mustang and drove across country. It was an adventure for us to go east to Indiana and for me to have him with me the first time I stepped foot on the campus of Notre Dame.

Although I was a priest and I was no longer of college age, I felt like a little kid on the first day of school. It was overwhelming. As it turned out, it was also one of the hottest summers Indiana had ever recorded.

I was put into a dorm with no air conditioning. I walked out of my room one night, and there sat a young man who I had seen in the hallways who I knew only by his first name. He was sobbing. So I leaned over him and said, "Are you okay?"

He looked up and said, "You know, I don't think I can take this anymore. The pressure is getting to me. I think I'm going to crack up with the demands."

He was just flattened by all he had to do – reports, projects, tests, and more papers. So I talked to him about where he was from, and learned he was from the south. I said to him, "You know, you don't have to put yourself through this. There's a good school in your state. So if this is stressing you out too much, you can know yourself, accept yourself, and respect your limitations. You can just transfer to another university at home."

When I said that, he looked up at me and then took both hands and wiped the tears from his face. He got to his feet and looked at me and said, "Are you crazy? I'm not going to leave Notre Dame. If I get through this, I'll get paid for it the rest of my life."

He walked back into his room, shut the door, and went back to work.

I look at my experiences at Notre Dame as being really life-changing in terms of human development. There were some simple things that I had never experienced before. And with any luck at all, I won't ever experience them again.

For instance, I got stuck in an elevator during a tornado, so I left Notre Dame with claustrophobia. And by the way if you're ever stuck in an elevator and think those phones are going to help you out, they don't. You pick one up, and you get a dial tone. Who do you call? Your mother? You're stuck on an elevator. In a tornado. Nobody's coming to get you. And back then, nobody would be carrying a cell phone for many more years.

Luckily, I managed to call the main operator for Notre Dame who sent their fire department out to free me. But the claustrophobia remains to this day.

In terms of my own human development, my days at Notre Dame really helped me learn how to be alone. Up until then, I had never spent much time by myself. I was always with people I knew.

It also helped me learn how to study. That may sound funny coming from somebody who had been in the seminary for eight years, but I learned different ways to study, and different ways to think. It helped me understand that there are liberal thoughts and conservative thoughts in the Catholic church, and you have to sift through them all to find the truth. You have to listen to what people are thinking.

There are also truths and untruths that come from all over. I remember one class I took on the sacraments, and the professor walked in – Fr. Regis Duffy – and he said, "I want to address one topic. Why do we have so many sacraments and so little faith?"

I knew he was a great scholar, but I was offended by the question. I raised my hand and said, "Father, working in a parish as a priest, I see a whole lot of faith out there with the people."

He said, "Really? What's your name?"

I said, "Dale."

"Where are you from?"

I responded, "Phoenix."

"Work in a parish?"

"Yes, a great parish."

He looked at me and said, "Good. But answer me one question, Dale-from-Phoenix. How many Mother Teresas do you have in your parish?"

I said, "Including me?"

"Including you."

"None."

He answered, "What's the difference in the communion that Mother Teresa receives, and the one that all the people in your parish receive? Why are there so many people who go to communion every Sunday and so little transformation that takes place?"

I was stunned. I realized he was right.

Catholics have a lot of sacraments. Catholics do a lot of baptisms, and have a lot of first communions and confirmations. Yet the churches are filled with people who are baptized yet uncatechized and who are often very un-Christian.

I began to develop a deeper sense of spirituality, and a deeper sense of what it's all about. In a very concrete way there were two things that the program at Notre Dame helped me come away with. The first was a greater love of worship. Catholics who read these words will better understand what I mean, and I don't want to get too holy and esoteric for non-Catholics who may be making their way through the book.

Understanding the incredible love that God has for us that He would come to us in such a humble way and in such a real way as in a piece of bread — that changed my passion.

Second, I gained a new vision of liturgy and worship of God as something that could no longer be separate from my daily life. I became convinced that liturgy and life had to start coming together if we were truly going to have the proper dignity that God wants us to have as human beings.

We have lost a sense of human dignity. I am not just talking about abortion, euthanasia, and issues of such essential concern. We have lost a general sense of respecting life in each other. And without that, we can't make decisions about the larger issues – the ones that go beyond us.

I think parents get so frazzled with child-care and running to soccer games that they forget that there is incredible human dignity in changing a child's diaper. It doesn't feel like it and it doesn't smell like it, but there is immense respect and compassion in caring for other human beings – especially our helpless children.

What I learned about human dignity is that the dignity comes from not what you do, but who you do it for.

I guess I always looked at jobs as having levels. Nobody seems to want the lower level ones like emptying the trash or cleaning house. What I found out is that in the old days your dignity came from not what your job was but whose household you came from.

So if you held a low level job for the king you were held in higher esteem than if you held a high level job for a lesser person.

If somebody says, "I'm a cook," you are inclined to say "That's nice."

But if somebody says, "I'm a cook at the White House," you say "wow" and are much more impressed.

What I began to comprehend is that God is so present in humanity that no matter what we're doing – if we're making a meal, setting up for a meeting – we're doing it for God. And that's where the dignity in the job comes from.

Those of us who struggle with self esteem and wonder what our lives are about, it's a matter of learning who we're working for. I learned that at Notre Dame.

Sometimes as I walked around the campus at night, I would look up at that golden dome and I would be overwhelmed. And there were other nights when I went to the library and I looked at the picture of the "Touchdown Jesus" and I'd think, "This is amazing."

Or I would go to the grotto where the students like to go to meditate and I would say a prayer. It was a deeply spiritual place, but I would say to myself, "What in the heck am I doing here? I'm a B-minus student from a middle income family in Phoenix, Arizona. What am I doing here at this university, praying in this grotto?"

I came to realize that it was a great unexpected gift from God to be there.

I sifted through issues for answers and I am sure I came to conclusions that the professors would have preferred that I not come to, and I am certain that I came to conclusions that others would not have agreed with.

I decided that if we could combine contemporary music and a live, spirit-filled liturgy and mix it with the Catholic church's traditions and teachings — and if we could say to people that the human condition and your daily struggles really matter, regardless of who you are — if we could take all these elements and mix them together we could change the world. When I finished the program at Notre Dame and Bishop O'Brien appointed me Vicar of Worship under his administration, I tried to deliver this message to the parishes throughout the diocese.

When I became pastor of St. Timothy's, that was my mission. Not everybody was happy about it, and many did not share my enthusiasm, to say the least. But despite that, a lot of people said things like, "Now my family and my life are holy. They have dignity. I can bring that to church, and I can come to church and the music is upbeat. I can sing the praises of God. I can combine my family, my job, my worship, and my faith and make it all work."

Graduating from Notre Dame helped my self esteem, there's no question about it. And once you graduate from Notre Dame, there is a loyalty that comes with the degree that is sort of hard to explain.

How Notre Dame changed my life was certainly unexpected. I found not only the presence of God in other people, but in my own heart as well.

CHAPTER 7
LIFE TEEN –
FROM DREAMING TO THE DREAM

When I was in the seminary, the very last thing I ever wanted to do was work with young people. I preferred mature adults.

In fact, I got into apostolic work, and for two years I visited a nursing home. I thought this was the greatest thing going. The older people were kind, and I remember there was a little lady named Gladys. She looked at me one day and said, "You know, I've wanted to be Roman Catholic for my entire life, and when I was younger my parents wouldn't let me. And then when I got married, my husband was a different religion and he wouldn't let me."

So I gave her catechism lessons, and she was brought into the Catholic church. I thought this was an amazing experience, and I truly believed I had found my life's work. I couldn't get over being part of an 85-year-old woman's dreams to become a Catholic.

Then I got assigned to teach a religious education class to teenagers in a home. And I was a disaster — an absolute and complete disaster.

I couldn't relate to these kids and I didn't know how to prepare material to teach them, so I just took the book and read to them and asked them the questions that were printed in the margins. Another seminarian and I were assigned to teach high school class in Camarillo on holiness, and as we drove down the road we kept stopping to let him puke because he had the flu. I said, "You can't go. You're sick."

So I took him back to the seminary and told him, "I will go to the first house and get them started, and then I will go to the second house and give them a project. I'll just go back and forth." I reassured him, "It will all be fine. I can cover it."

Believe me, it wasn't fine.

I went to the first house to get them started, and then I went to my assigned house. When I returned to the first house I discovered that there were no adults there, and instead of doing the assignments I had given them, the kids had gotten into the liquor cabinet and started drinking.

I'll tell you what, the next day I got called by the sister who was in charge, and I really thought I was going to be kicked out of the seminary. She was furious that I had left these kids alone, but I really didn't know what else to do. She wanted to kill me.

The only bright spot in the whole class was a kid named Alan – a nice looking, athletic kid who read the bible. So I read through the catechism books and asked questions, Alan would always raise his hand because he knew the answers. He was a lifesaver, and told me he was thinking about becoming a priest.

I went back to Phoenix for the summer. On the first day I returned to California in the fall, I was in the local Ralph's grocery store and I ran into Alan's mother. She said, "Oh Dale, you have to come to the house for dinner."

If you've ever tasted seminary food, you know that receiving a dinner invitation is like getting a reprieve. I said, "You name it, and I'll be there."

But she said, "Well, it won't be entirely social because Alan has left the Catholic church. He's started attending another church, and we really don't know what to make of the whole situation."

So I went to their home for dinner, and right after dessert the entire family stood up and left, except for Alan. I said, "Alan, how are you?"

"Fine."

I said, "So what's going on?"

He answered, "You know what's going on. That's why you're here."

I said, "That's right. I understand you're not Catholic anymore."

"That's right."

"Why?"

He put his head back down in the strawberry shortcake and kept eating.

I said, "Alan, look at me."

So he looked up and I said, "Is it the pope? Do you have trouble with the pope?"

He said, "Nope. The pope seems like a pretty nice guy to me."

I thought a second, and then asked, "Is it the moral teachings of the church? You having trouble with those?" I thought maybe he had been fooling around with a girlfriend over the summer and was having second thoughts.

He answered, "No, those are right out of the bible."

I said, "Is it the eucharist? Are you having trouble believing that it's really the body of Christ?"

He said, "No that's in the bible, too. 'This is my body.' It's right there."

I asked, "Does your new church believe in that?"

He said, "I don't know. They've never mentioned it."

I went on. "Wait a minute. You believe in the pope and you believe in the teachings of the church and you believe in the eucharist, but you don't even know if this new group you belong to believes in the eucharist? Why not?"

Alan looked at me and said, "Dale, for 16 years of my life never once did I miss mass, and never once did I feel loved. I don't know what this new church believes, but I know they love me."

That was a life-changing moment for me. I wanted to say, "We love you. The church loves you."

But how could I say that to someone whose experience for 16 years – in Alan's case, it was a lifetime – had been the opposite? So I decided that if and when I became a priest, I was going to put energy into young people. Little did I know that later in life, after three decades of ministry, I would become Alan.

When I became associate pastor of St. Jerome's Parish in Phoenix, I started a group. My pastor, Monsignor Richard Moyer, was extremely supportive. He's very German and one might think the kids wouldn't have related to him, but they loved him. Somehow when he was with them, he just opened up and accepted them, and they responded.

When I was transferred from there and moved in with the bishop, I was assigned to a parish called St. Louis the King. I called a couple of other parishes in the area trying to sell them on the idea of a group for young people. There was an old monsignor at one parish that I called six times to ask if I could come in to his parish and start a youth group. He finally called back and said, "No, our kids aren't interested in religion."

He was right.

I did work with young people at St. Louis the King, and in 1985 I became pastor of St. Timothy's in Mesa. My first day at the parish I said to the people, "What you hear from this pulpit is going to be authentically Catholic. It's not going to be my opinion. And I am going to go after your teens, and I'm going to go after the high school across the street."

Those were my goals. And of course, if you have goals like that, you have to have back-up and committed partners. My first was Phil Baniewicz.

Phil was a young man whom I had known briefly at St. Jerome's, and then he had gone to St. Louis the King with me to help start the youth group there. He was exceptionally gifted and really loved God, but he also had the ability to love other people. He became like a son to me.

The truth is that although I got a lot of the credit for Life Teen, Phil Baniewicz should be credited with its success. He worked much harder than I did, and with more talent. The Catholic church owes Phil a great debt.

We decided we needed a musician. I remembered that when I had been deacon, I had met a young man with long, scraggly hair named Tom Booth. Periodically, I still had contact with him. Soon after I made pastor, Tom came to see me and asked if he could go to confession. Tom was a rock musician with a great heart, and he came in to see me to lay his burdens down, so to speak.

The poor guy would tell me a sin, and I would say, "Okay, but do you have health insurance?" Then he'd tell me another sin, and I would say, "Okay, but do you know what you're going to do with your career?"

By the end of the confession, I had not only offered him absolution, I had also offered him a job. I can't break the seal of the confessional and tell you what his sins had been, but I can tell you that he worked for me for more than two decades. So you can only imagine what the penance was. He was an amazing musician.

The three of us, along with an original core group of people, started a group that we called Life Teen. Soon after we began, a man named Tom Ryan approached us and said, "This is too good. You have to put this on television."

We made a pilot program, and sent it to Mother Angelica at EWTN. Within two days, the station called us back and said, "We want this on the air."

We began producing a weekly program for youth on Catholic television. Mother Angelica flew out to Phoenix, and I still have a great picture of her standing at the altar in the sanctuary with her arms around a couple of kids, swaying.

Life Teen started to grow. And as it started to grow, people had a variety of reactions. A newspaper called The Wanderer thought it was evil incarnate. Other media sources referred to Life Teen as awesome. Some pastors thought it was a fad, and others thought it was an answer to reaching out to the young people in their parishes.

A good man named Dan Ketcherside came to me and said, "You need to get a board of directors, and take Life Teen to the next level."

Although over the years it has been a struggle for me to deal with a board of directors and all that it entails, I will also tell you that some of the finest human beings I have ever met are people who have served on this board – doctors, lawyers, and other faith-filled people.

What we all came to understand is that the Catholic church has lost two and probably three generations of its youth. There are lots of reasons for this — the plight of Catholic education and how expensive it has become, the decline in priests, the decline in sisters

A book called Soul Searching was released by an author named Christian Smith. It takes a look at the spiritual and religious life of American teenagers. There is a section about Catholics, and fundamentally what he comes up with is that, with the exception of our Jewish brothers and sisters, nobody has done a worse job of reaching their youth than Catholics. This is primarily because it has not been a real priority for us.

Having said that, I will say that Pope John Paul II did everything he could to change that perspective. His World Youth Days, the frequency with which he spoke directly to young people and his openness with them all revealed his love for them.

But a 75 year old man in Rome cannot be a youth minister. He inspired people, but it is a simple truth that a large number of the people who flocked to Rome to see him were not necessarily buying into what he was saying, even though they bought into him.

So we started a program in 1985 called Life Teen, and through word of mouth and EWTN it started to grow until it became a movement in the Catholic church. At World Youth Day in Denver in 1993 with the pope, amazing things took place. Wonderful things continued to happen.

In 2000 I was in Rome for World Youth Day, and on the Spanish steps when the eucharist was brought out. Fifteen thousand people fell to their knees. It is something I will never forget.

Life Teen continued to attract attention because of the impact it had on the lives of teenagers. People from all over the world started asking what was going on and how they could reach their young people.

The fundamentals are basic: You have to make it a priority. You have to devote time, money, and labor to reaching our youth. I am really humbled at what has happened with Life Teen. When I left Catholic ministry, they had grown the program to about 1,000 parishes. Some join, some lose interest and drop off, which is all part of the process. But the upward climb is steady.

Life Teen is currently found in many foreign countries – Australia, New Zealand, Mexico, Canada, Great Britain. Now that sounds a little more impressive in some cases than it really is, because in some countries it's just a parish here or there that have the program going.

But there are three camps. Cove Crest is in Atlanta where Jack Busche, Glenn Mayer, and Randy Rouse have done an incredible job of taking a camp and making it a light.

There is a camp now in St. Louis named RockyVine. One of the board members, Pat Barron, is an amazing man with an amazing vision.

Here in Arizona, Life Teen bought a camp from the diocese. Nicole Bidwill and Monsignor Richard Moyer were instrumental in making it all come together.

In addition, they have an incredible website. Matt Smith who is the webmaster was originally on MTV with The Real World. And let me tell you, I was criticized up and down for daring to make somebody a spokesperson for Life Teen who had been on MTV. It created quite a controversy and I was chewed up and spit out over and over again. Yet the second show Matt did, he wore a Life Teen tee shirt the entire time. Life Teen could never have afforded to buy that kind of advertising.

Somebody else set the precedent for this kind of marketing, though. And the chairman of his board is pretty impressive, too. Christ went out into the marketplace where everybody was, including the sinners. He didn't wait for the sinners to come to him.

My vision was, if we can get somebody from MTV to talk about Life Teen — which Matt did — and to talk about Christ, which Matt did — the message would reach kids we would never find otherwise. MTV was mainstream culture, and like it or not, most young people want to be a part of what is current.

Kids absolutely loved Matt Smith, and we didn't just stop with him. We got some other great, talented people like Mark Hart to help us start a studio. We put in first-class cameras and editing equipment so we could make films and videos to reach the kids.

We also found some other incredible folks throughout the country to help. A young musician named Matt Maher came to work for St. Tim's and Life Teen. Today he is wonderfully successful in contemporary Christian music. Matt has been a loyal friend and I believe the most gifted songwriter since Rich Mullins died.

When people ask me if I ever expected that this whole movement is what Life Teen would become, I answered, "I didn't think youth ministry was so bad in the church that Life Teen would have to become this big. But it is."

When you say that the Life Teen program is in 1,000 parishes, it sounds like a great many. However, there are 19,000 Catholic parishes in the United States alone. They are really just scratching the surface.

One of the great partners in youth ministry was Franciscan

University in Steubenville, Ohio. I was at a conference there one time facilitated by Fr. Mike Scanlon and Fr. Dave Pivanka, who both have a great love of young people and who possess great vision.

At a mass I did, I said "I love you" after the sign of peace. Afterwards, a priest came up to me and started yelling at me. He said, "Who cares who you love? How dare you say that! It doesn't say that in the book! You're supposed to be praying out of the book!"

I looked at him as young people stood all around listening to him yell at me. I said, "Sir, I think you're reading out of the wrong book. The book that I read, which is the sacred scripture, tells us that we are supposed to express love."

Some people become so rigid that having a celebrant tell them that he loves them – and remember he should be the incarnation of Christ's love – becomes offensive.

Youth ministry is very hard under the best of circumstances, but it is truly difficult in light of all the scandals, both in and out of the Catholic church. Some people want to assume that you are in youth ministry for all the wrong reasons, and some highly qualified, good-hearted people don't want any part of youth ministry because of the potential risk that is involved in youth ministry. Regardless, it is still life-changing to work with youth because of the energy they have.

Once when I got off a plane in St. Louis a young man walked up to and said, "Aren't you Fr. Dale?"

I said, "Yes."

He said, "You saved my life."

I said, "Really?" I was somewhat taken off guard and unsure as to what he really wanted from me.

He continued, "No, I really mean it. You saved my life. I recognized you from the videos at Life Teen. I tried to commit suicide but failed. And while I was in the hospital recovering, a friend of mine came to see me and told me that when I got out of there I was going to church with him. I got involved in Life Teen, and for the first time in my life, I had meaning. So thank you."

With that, he walked off, and I stood there watching him disappear into the crowd.

When I was in Cleveland at a conference, a young girl stood up and talked about being depressed and suicidal and how becoming involved in the Catholic church and Life Teen changed her life. She said, "I found a place where somebody really cared about me."

I have had young people tell me about drugs and alcohol, and things much worse than that. All the work, all of the pain, and all of the money that have gone into Life Teen are worth every drop of sweat and every penny for just one of the kids it has reached out for and changed.

The truth is, there are thousands of kids out there whose names I will never know, who have had their lives enriched. No matter what happens in my life – ups, downs, accusations, accolades – nobody can ever take away the fact that there are young people who found hope and young people who found a welcome in the church.

My goal, no matter what happens to me, is to make sure that nobody of any age walks away from Christ because he or she didn't feel loved.

I used to say that Martin Luther King had a dream. I couldn't imitate him, so I proclaimed that I had a "scheme." My scheme was to revolutionize the church by making young people so alive in faith that they would change the landscape of religion.

The dream and the scheme were taken away from me.

I love a book called Primal by Mark Patterson. While reading it, I came across the following story, on page 195. My jaw dropped, because it seems to describe me:

"I recently met Phil Vischer, the creator of Veggie Tales. It was sort of surreal hearing the voice of Bob The Tomato in nonanimated form. But Phil is as likable as the characters he created.

Phil started out with loose change and grew Big Idea Inc. into a multimillion-dollar company that has sold more than fifty million videos. Over a three-year span during its heyday, revenues grew from $1.3 million to $44 million – that's an increase of 3,300 percent. But that all came to an end with one lawsuit. As Phil himself said, 'Fourteen year's worth of work flashed before my eyes – the characters, the songs, the impact, the letters from kids all over the world. It all flashed before my eyes, then it all vanished'

Big Idea declared bankruptcy. The dream died. And Phil was left to do some serious soul-searching. That's when Phil heard a sermon that saved his soul and changed his life. 'If God gives you a dream, and the dream comes to life and God shows up in it, and the dream dies, it may be that God wants to see what is more important to you – the dream or him.'"

CHAPTER 8
THE TRUTH WILL SET YOU FREE

In 1995, I was accused of sexual harassment by a former employee in his late twenties. I didn't know what sexual harassment was until I found myself accused of it.

What I think took place is that I regarded this man as somebody who was absolutely a member of my inner circle of friends. He was somebody I took in too quickly to this most private part of my life.

When he took his accusations to the diocese, he met with the diocesan representatives numerous times. I don't know specifically how the entire process worked, but eventually the diocese sent a letter saying that there was no sexual harassment involved.

For me, it was all very painful, embarrassing and dark. Ultimately, the case settled for $45,000 — a third of which supposedly went to the man's attorney, and two-thirds went to him. I am certain the diocese settled because it would have cost hundreds of thousands of dollars to fight the case, and it would have been difficult and painful for many people besides me. Part of the settlement entailed a document that the man signed promising not to reveal any of the terms or details.

I never had to sign a similar document, but the diocese did. Several years later after a case came to light involving a youth worker at a parish who was arrested for molesting a young man, somebody notified the Chandler police department of the prior settlement involving me, and it was included in the police report and therefore became public knowledge.

I then publicly acknowledged that the episode had taken place and that there had been a settlement. I never revealed any of the details, and I never used the man's name. To this day I still have not.

In fact, after the settlement was made, the man came back to mass and told me that it was over, that he was ready to move on. I apologized for whatever pain I might have caused him. That is the last time I saw him. For a couple of years in a row, I even got a Christmas card from him.

As a Notre Dame graduate, I am a big Notre Dame football fan. And even though Notre Dame hadn't had a great season, they were invited to the Insight.com Bowl in Phoenix. It was played after Christmas in December 2004.

All of this doesn't sound terribly significant, except I was on my way to the football game with a priest friend of mine when I got a call from one of the men who had replaced me as vicar general that an allegation had been made against me and I needed to come in to the chancery office immediately.

It was late afternoon, and I went down to meet him at the chancery. The new vicar general informed me that a man had come forward and had notified the diocese via a letter from his attorney that he would be filing a suit against me and against the diocese for an alleged event that had supposedly occurred in the summer of 1985.

The vicar general was diplomatic, but as he told me the nature of the allegation, I literally began to laugh at the absurdity of it. When the vicar general told me the name of the accuser, I was in absolute shock.

The gist of this man's story is that we got him drunk at the rectory, and that a seminarian (who was working there for the summer and eventually spent 10 years in prison for molesting a couple of girls), and our youth minister (who was extremely gifted but homophobic) assaulted him as I watched. The story continued that I never touched him but went off into a corner alone to masturbate. This scene was supposedly repeated on a number of occasions.

There were many flaws in the story. One, I rarely if ever consume alcohol. Two, the accuser had never been to the rectory for dinner when he was a kid. Three, I never witnessed anybody engaged in anything of this nature in my life. Four, the other person being accused – the youth minister – was the last person on the face of the universe who would have been involved in something like this. And five, the man had supposedly forgotten about it all for 20 years and had just "remembered" it.

Having said all that, it turned out to not be at all funny, despite my initial inclination to laugh. What the diocese did is to turn the matter over to the county attorney.

I think it quite odd that this man and his attorney didn't go to the county attorney themselves. What they did is go to the diocese with a letter to say that they were going to follow it with a lawsuit.

When a lawyer does something of this nature, he's not being polite in issuing a warning. What he is doing is trying to get a reaction: "Oh, please don't do that. How much money will it take to make this go away?"

Certainly the diocese called the bluff. One, they turned it over to the county attorney. And two, they made no gestures of settlement.

That first meeting with the vicar general, I offered immediately to take a polygraph test. I am certain this is what the diocese should have had me do to see if there was any credibility to the accusations. But they blew it off, and I believe honestly they could not wait to announce the allegations to the media. They called a press conference so quick it would have made your head spin. They also informed me that I was on leave of absence, and I needed to get out of the parish.

What had happened during the whole sex scandal affair was that there were allegations and accusations about bishops not taking sexual abuse seriously enough. Bishops were accused of moving priests around to avoid prosecution, and so forth. What has happened now is that the pendulum has swung so far the other direction that few reasonable, rational, or human considerations are being given to priests accused of misconduct.

That first fateful night after my initial meeting, I went on to the football game and waited to hear back from the diocese. After the fourth quarter was over, I got a call telling me to get out of St. Timothy's immediately.

What you need to understand is that when you remove a priest from ministry, you aren't just removing him from a job. It's not just like getting fired. If IBM lets you go, you still have the rest of your life.

When I left, it seemed to 5,000 families and 100 staff members that some alien ship had arrived to abduct me and lift me up and out of everything.

I was taken out of my home, my community, my environment, and my work all because somebody said that 20 years ago when he was 14 years old that a series of terrible events occurred that he forgot about for a couple of decades.

If you read about repressed memories, what is said is that they can happen when you are very young because you don't have the tools and the perspective to comprehend what has happened to you. But when you are 14 years old, if you are raped – and raped a number of times – your issue is not that you can't remember what happened. Your issue is that you can't get it off your mind.

You deal with it every day of your life. A young woman who is raped may not tell anybody about it, but she is not going to forget about it. She isn't going to NOT remember.

The way the law is written about these things is that the clock on the statute of limitations starts ticking from the moment you remember, not from the moment the actual events took place. Interestingly enough, this man had gone to the county attorney about the seminarian who had allegedly raped him, but said nothing about the youth minister or me because he supposedly hadn't remembered that part of the story yet. It took him another two years. Clearly, what we were being propelled by is his attorney's desire for money.

These outlandish alleged repressed memories were supposedly recovered by a counselor from the church next door who had no certification in dealing with repressed memories and was in way over her head. However, one reality about repressed memories is that you can plant something in somebody's mind, and soon they won't be able to tell what is real and what isn't.

The accusations were absolutely and totally false. Yet, even seven months later, the Maricopa County attorney's office still hadn't talked to me, hadn't talked to the youth minister, had not talked to the seminarian, and had not talked to my attorney.

I have the best attorney in the state of Arizona, as far as I am concerned. Michael Manning is respected nationwide as a man of integrity and of brilliance. Yet even with him representing me, we knew nothing more after many weeks of waiting.

The diocese said that it was trying to hurry the process along, but I have information from someone in the county attorney's office that the opposite was true. They were not trying to hurry the process along. Instead, they cited the situation as an example to a group called S.N.A.P. (Survivors Network of Those Abused by Priests) to illustrate that the bishop was not going to play favorites.

I was approached by a representative of the diocese about resigning from the parish of St. Timothy's, where I had served as pastor for 20 years. It is something I did not want to do, but it was clear that the bishop and the diocese wanted me to do it so the parish could move on.

So I resigned. Again, everything was all over the news that I resigned for the good of the parish. But it wasn't interpreted that way.

I asked to take a lie detector test, and finally paid several hundred dollars of my own money to take it. Talk about things you never expected to do in your lifetime. I never envisioned myself sitting in a chair with bands around my stomach, my arms, and my fingers and somebody else sitting in a chair trying to determine whether or not I was lying. A lie detector test, a polygraph, is incredibly demeaning and stressful.

Some people question the validity of the polygraph, but almost everybody in law enforcement agrees that there is a degree of accuracy to them. The better the person you have operating and reading the tests, the better the results are. I waited for a month for an ex-FBI agent who had taught at Quantico how to administer the lie detector test. He is considered the best in Arizona, and probably the best in the country.

I was asked a lot of unrelated questions, and I tried to be absolutely truthful. The one question that threw me for a loop was a yes or no question: "Did you ever take credit for academic work that wasn't yours when you were in the seminary?"

I ultimately answered no, because I couldn't think of anything specific after so many years. But I wanted to answer "probably" because when I was in a study group or something similar in college, I undoubtedly had borrowed from other people's work or thinking. Almost every college student does that. But I couldn't think of anything in particular, despite wracking my brains. I tried to decide what to answer, yes or no.

But they asked me three relevant questions among all the other ones about this issue: Did I participate in the sexual abuse of this kid? Did I give him alcohol? Did I have any knowledge of these events?

On a lie detector test, you can have three results: pass, fail, or inconclusive. On two of the questions on the first round, I passed. On the third question, it was a pass but was nearing inconclusive. So they asked if I would be willing to do a whole other round, which I did.

That time, the man who administered the test said that I had hit home runs, that it was clear I was telling the truth.

The New Times did an article about me where they gathered up a vast amount of information and made me look like I was an absolute monster. I will say that when your premise starts with a lie, the outcome is going to be a lie. Garbage in, garbage out.

My friend, Fr. Jack Spaulding, was appointed pastor of St. Timothy's. In a weird twist of reality, I actually went shopping with him for furniture so he could move into the house and office I occupied for more than 20 years.

People at the parish continued to be supportive; people at the diocesan level continued to offer no support. I believe that there are people at the diocese who hoped the allegations were true.

But the facts of the situation are these: the pendulum has swung so far the other way that as a human being my rights and my dignity were absolutely taken away from me. I think I now understand more about what prejudice is. When a person of color goes into certain neighborhoods, he or she is immediately suspect. When a case goes to the county attorney, if you have a certain occupation you are treated differently than any other citizen would be treated because you are a Catholic priest.

My life changed forever. My job, my home, my career, my family, my finances, and my future have all been changed because of an incredible lie.

Although the people who know me and love me have stood by me, and even people who don't know me who read the stories and shook their heads and said, "This is too far-fetched" – it has still been excruciatingly painful.

The faith of the Catholic church changed for me, too. I say to myself, "Even if everything this person is claiming was true and did happen, where and who is the face of Christ for me? Who in the diocese — what bishop, what person would say to me 'you are still a child of God'?"

I am still in a state of disbelief that I can go from making decisions that helped guide the Diocese of Phoenix for years and years to being someone that is so expendable to the Catholic hierarchy and to the Catholic church.

I find it very difficult to comprehend how the Catholic church can wage a fight to respect the life that is in a womb and not respect people who are already born. This includes prisoners, people who do things we don't like or agree with. Where is the face of Christ?

People asked me, "What do you want to have happen; what do you hope takes place?"

They often inquired if I wanted to become pastor of another Catholic parish, and I said in all honesty, "no." At the time I began writing this book, I was still in a state of limbo. I know the Catholic church no longer believes in limbo, but believe me I was in it and the Catholic church created it.

People still question me about how I want things to end, and I always reply with the same answer: Someday I want this man to tell the truth. Not the truth as he wished it had happened, not the truth that his attorney hoped happened so that he could get into the diocese's pockets, and not the truth that the counselor planted in his mind – but the actual truth.

The truth is what it is. These events never took place. But I was treated as if they had, and I will continue to be regarded with suspicion by some people. Many would call that injustice. I simply call it my new reality.

CHAPTER 9
A NEW BISHOP FOR PHOENIX

When the new millennium hit, my life changed. I was appointed Vicar General of the Diocese of Phoenix.

When people hear the term "vicar general" they have no clue as to what that means. They don't know what "vicar" means — its basic definition is somebody who stands in the place of somebody else — and they encounter the word "general" and they assume it's a military term. In the Catholic church, the vicar general stands in the place of the bishop — generally. What that means is that as vicar general, you have the bishop's authority in every area of the diocese that he wants you to use it.

It is unlike the vice president of a corporation or company in that the vicar general is not the second in command because clearly in the Catholic church the bishop is the one ordained to be a successor of the apostles. So you have no authority as a vicar general unless the bishop gives it to you.

In our diocese, a great man, priest, and friend — Monsignor Richard Moyer — had served as vicar general for 20 years. The way that Bishop Thomas O'Brien utilized Msgr. Moyer was in the areas of finance and administration. After the new millennium began, Bishop O'Brien decided he was going to appoint a second vicar general, which is something that canon law allows.

I can still remember exactly what happened. I was at an ecumenical meeting at 7:00 a.m. and the bishop was there, too. I was hosting the meeting, I had been unable to sleep the night before, and I was just exhausted. I facilitated the meeting, and as people were leaving Bishop O'Brien said, "May I see you for a minute?"

I said, "Certainly. Let me see everybody to the door and say goodbye, and I will be right with you."

I said my farewells, and then the bishop and I took a seat in a quiet corner of the room. He said, "Will you be my vicar general?"

I said, "Yes. Starting when?"

He replied, "Starting now." He made the announcement that afternoon.

He made it very clear to me what my areas of responsibility were to be. Primarily, I was to be in charge of building a new diocesan pastoral center, which included raising $15 million and overseeing the entire huge project. Staff had to be moved out of the old buildings, the old structures had to be knocked down, new plans had to be drawn up, funding had to be generated for the new building, the construction had to be overseen, and then when everything was completed the staff had to be moved back in. All of this activity would take place in downtown Phoenix.

The bishop had a vision that he wanted a big plaza, so we had to talk the city into giving us a street, closing off another street, and letting us knock down an historic building. It was a battle from start to finish, but it was also a joy to see something so beautiful sprout up downtown.

I thought getting the center built was a very bloody battle, but I had no notion as to what was to come.

As vicar general, I had no input into how priest personnel issues were handled. I had no input as to how sexual misconduct issues were addressed. Concerns of this nature came under the auspices of the chancellor and a team of professionals who handled such issues. I was not on this team and was not privy to how the processes worked.

When the national sex scandal broke, especially in Boston and throughout the eastern part of the country, a local reporter proclaimed Phoenix to be the second worst diocese in the country for hiding sex scandals. It was an irresponsible statement not just because it was inflammatory, but because it was blatantly untrue.

I was told later by an undeniably reliable and impeccable source that a high profile Phoenix newspaper and its local television affiliate held a meeting to plan how they were going to "expose" Bishop O'Brien and bring him down. It was also stated at the meeting that they knew they would have to bring me down as well.

It sounds rather bizarre, and I have no doubt that these particular reporters and so-called journalists would deny that these events took place. But I also have no doubt that they happened. I am certain that the intention of at least some of the local media was to create a change in the Catholic diocese.

For many years, Bishop O'Brien was loved. He was always viewed as a good man, and a kind man. There is no question that as the diocese got bigger and bigger, it became more difficult to manage.

Once the dam broke nationally with the sex scandal and it flowed into the local channels here, what we had was chaos in the diocese. The media coverage was absolutely relentless and unbelievably sensationalistic about the bishop, about individual priests, and about me.

In the midst of it all, a youth minister who worked at St. Timothy's was arrested for molesting a kid, and the media attempted to convey the impression that I knew what was happening. I truly never suspected sexual abuse was taking place in my parish, and certainly not at the hands of one of my employees.

The youth minister lived with the family of the victim for four years, and they didn't know, either. They saw him day in and day out, and his actions never revealed anything to alarm them or make them suspicious of his treatment of their son.

When the situation became known, it was pandemonium. There were information leaks among the clergy – anything that was said at a priests' meeting or at the diocese was immediately leaked to the press. There were even times when we believed the phones were tapped.

Maricopa County Attorney Rick Romley literally took control of the situation – a move that created even more controversy. My role during all of this had nothing to do with addressing the particulars of the individual cases, but was to assemble some prominent Catholic leaders to form a crisis management team that would help us swim through the sharks in the ocean. Some very fine and competent people assisted us.

We ultimately resorted to enlisting the services of a fine public relations firm because the general public was being affected by the onslaught of negative stories they heard about the Catholic church and its clergy every time they turned on their television sets.

Then the worst of all possible scenarios occurred.

I was getting ready for an evening mass, and I ran over to my room in the rectory to use the bathroom. My cell phone rang. It was the gentleman we had hired to be the building manager at the diocesan pastoral center. He had called to tell me that the police had been at the center to search for a vehicle that had been involved in a fatal hit and run accident. The car had been traced to an auto dealer, and from there to the diocese.

It was clear to me that the accident involved one of only a couple of people who had cars acquired through the particular dealership. Because of the location, it would either have to have been Bishop O'Brien or the priest who was the rector at Ss. Simon and Jude Cathedral.

Right before I began mass, I called the police officer who was the contact person for the investigation into the accident. He explained to me that somebody had died at the scene, and asked if I knew who the car belonged to. I said, "I don't know if it's the bishop's car or the monsignor's car, and I don't know where the bishop is right now."

I told the officer I would try to locate the bishop immediately after mass. He said he would expect my call.

One of the hardest things I have ever had to do in my life was to go before 1,500 people — 500 of whom were teenagers — and celebrate mass. We were praising God and I was trying to present everything as being wonderful and joyful, and all the time I was thinking to myself, "If this was the bishop, all hell is going to break loose."

After mass, I tried to call the bishop, and got no response. So I called the police officer back, and he said, "We want to see the car."

After I provided the police with the bishop's address, I believed my goal was to find the bishop and talk him into going home so he could meet with the police. I called his sister's house, and got the bishop on the phone and told him about my conversation with the police officer.

I said to him, "Bishop, a man died."

There was a long pause, and he replied, "Oh my God."

I continued, "The police want you to go home so they can see your car."

He confirmed to me that he had been driving, that he had hit something, and there was damage to his car.

The irony is that he was driving the car around, and had made no attempt to hide it. He drove it to mass the morning after the accident, then he drove it to his sister's house and parked it in front of the house. I think that what people don't understand is that when you are under siege, as he was with the priest sex scandal, your mind works in very different ways than are normal.

I think that the bishop's initial reaction sums it all up. He said his first thought was, "How did they know I was going to be driving down this particular street?"

I believe in my heart of hearts that Bishop O'Brien truly believed that somebody was out after him. There had been death threats against him, and I think his instinct was to get home where he would be safe in a secure environment.

I had talked to him previously on many occasions about having somebody travel with him so that he would never be in a situation like this. I kept calling the bishop's house on that Sunday night to no avail, and in my mind I kept picturing him going home and meeting with the police. The next morning, the police were there, and started interviewing him and it was all over the media. The hell that I feared would break loose totally erupted.

The police decided to arrest the bishop for hit and run. Seeing my bishop being taken into jail was unbelievable. In fact, when they took him in his heartbeat became so erratic that they had to transport him to St. Joseph's Hospital. I went down and anointed him in case he was having a heart attack.

I will never in my life forget the night when he was bailed out. Kim Sue Lia-Perkes, our diocesan communications director, was there and there had to have been 75 reporters crowded around. Kim Sue and I went downtown to pick up the bishop, and I drove a rental car because mine had been taken in to be serviced. She opened the car to get into the back seat, and the reporters literally lay on the vehicle with their cameras trying to get inside to take photos. The car was shaking up and down. Inmates and passersby were screaming out of the prison, and reporters were yelling. I sat there ready to drive away as soon as Kim Sue got the bishop safely into the car, which seemed an almost impossible task. It was a nightmare that I couldn't ever imagine I would be living.

As I drove, reporters stood in front of the car to try to block our exit so they could get pictures. Here I was with my bishop who had been charged with hitting somebody, and I was afraid to move for fear that I would do the same thing. Some sheriff's deputies tried to hold back the crowd so we could get out, and a few followed us to try to assist us at the other end of the ride back to the bishop's house so we could get him safely out of the car. There were people everywhere when we arrived, and it was a repeat of the scene we had just left.

It was an unreal situation to be in.

The next morning, I went to visit the bishop and his family. As I left to return home, I got a call from my secretary who said, "Where are you?"

I said, "I'm just leaving the bishop's house."

She said, "The papal nuncio from Washington, D.C. just called. He needs to speak to you immediately. He is sitting next to the phone waiting for you to call."

I started shaking. I was literally one minute away from the bishop's house, and I pulled off to the side of the road and wrote down the number my secretary repeated to me. I was also sadly naive about electronics, and thought a cell phone was a safe means to have a private conversation.

A white van had followed me, and pulled off to the side when I did. Later when I returned home after completing the heartbreaking tasks of the day, it was quite clear that my conversation with the papal nuncio had been overheard and the contents divulged to the media. The news channels blazed with rhetoric, and the headlines in the newspaper were scathing.

I called the papal nuncio and he asked kindly how we were doing and how Bishop O'Brien was doing. I told him that we were doing as well as could be expected under the circumstances. He then told me that the Holy Father, Pope John Paul II, had asked him to call me to convey to the bishop that the Holy Father would receive his resignation. I felt the blood leave my face.

He asked me how far away I was from the bishop's house. I told him less than two minutes, and he told me to go back immediately and have the conversation with the bishop. The papal nuncio was very kind and very concerned about the welfare of the diocese, the bishop, and me. But he also invited no discussion. I had to do as I was commanded, however gently the command had been issued.

I returned to the bishop's house to inform him as to what had happened. Here was a man who I served, and I had to tell him that he had to resign.

But he wasn't ready to resign. Certainly he was numb, but he finally signed a paper that I wrote out saying that he resigned as

Bishop of Phoenix, effective the next day.

We then called the papal nuncio, and the bishop said reluctantly that he offered his resignation. It was so incredibly painful for both of us that I have difficulty thinking about it even now.

Within minutes, I was speaking to Archbishop Michael Sheehan from Santa Fe with whom the papal nuncio had already made arrangements to take over the diocese. I can't say enough good things about him. His presence was healing, he was honest and forthright, and he brought a sense of humor and of hope when he arrived.

I wish I could say that the story – although a sad one – ends here. Unfortunately, that is not the case. Not long after, I was called to what seemed like an endless string of meetings with attorneys, and ultimately had to testify against my bishop, Thomas J. O'Brien, by simply telling what had happened.

He wasn't drinking, as some people tried to portray, or doing any of those kinds of things. I believe firmly that we were all in such a state of chaos that something bad had to come out of it.

The man who walked across the street and walked into the bishop's car was drunk. The bishop did not realize that he had hit a person. There was no indifference on the part of the bishop in hitting him and leaving him there. They were both part of a senseless tragedy.

If life had been proceeding normally and the bishop hadn't been operating from a state of siege mentality, if he had stopped and prayed over this man as he died, the bishop would have been perceived in a very different light, maybe even as a hero. But certainly as a more sympathetic player in a tragic human drama.

Negativity would have been hard to harbor against such a man. But he wasn't thinking clearly. The seriousness of what had happened did not register with him.

He didn't hit the pedestrian on purpose, and I don't believe he left the man behind on purpose. I believe that because of all the terrible things that were going on as a result of the clergy sex scandal, Bishop O'Brien fled looking for sanctuary.

When Archbishop Sheehan arrived, the first thing he asked me is, "Who is going to the funeral at the Indian reservation?"

I said, "Archbishop, we spoke to our attorneys and they didn't think it was a good idea."

He looked at me and then said at 9:00 at night, "I don't care if they don't think it's a good idea. You need to go and pray with that family."

So I called my dear friend Johnny Basha and asked, "Johnny, may I borrow an airplane?"

Within minutes, he arranged to fly four of us up to the reservation to attend the funeral and pray with the family.

To this day, I don't know how they received it, but I know it was the right thing to do. That was the great lesson that Archbishop Sheehan taught us.

At the end of the trial, the bishop was convicted and given 1,000 hours of community service and a suspended sentence. But what I saw was this good man had been destroyed as a human being.

There is no question that when you are in leadership you are torn when you have to make decisions. I don't think that Bishop O'Brien always got the best legal advice during his more than 20 years as our bishop. However, I know that he always desired the good of the Catholic church and the good of the people of Phoenix.

Frequently I think that people don't remember the incredible things that this man did. He is the one who brought Pope John Paul II to Phoenix. He is the one who brought Mother Teresa to Phoenix. He was at the helm during the unprecedented growth of the diocese.

Today, Bishop O'Brien has his sense of humor back. He will never recover from the events of the past, but he is still loved and received warmly wherever he goes. My personal affection for him is strong and in the midst of my own nightmare that eventually surrounded me, he remained a Christian, a friend, and a sign of God's love. He was and is a good and decent man.

About six months after the initial flurry of tragedies, we got word that the Vatican had announced a new bishop, Bishop Thomas Olmsted. He came among us described as being a prayerful man who had a very different vision of church.

Over the past several years, Thomas Olmsted has not been received well by the people of Phoenix as their bishop. He is distant from the people, not ecumenical, uncaring, and is perceived by many as being a man of "rules," and not a man of Christ.

Recently at a hospital I ran into a spiritual leader from another denomination. His first words to me were, "How is that son of a bitch who is running the diocese?"

In my own situation, Thomas Olmsted became a symbol of all that is wrong with the institution of the Catholic church. He excommunicates, not reconciles. He evaluates rules and rubrics and cares little about spirituality. He has also caused a tremendous decrease in funding for the diocese because the people, in general, do not like him.

At one time, the Diocese of Phoenix was the envy of Catholics around the country. Life Teen, alive liturgies, tremendous growth, great diocesan activities, and hope for the future were the hallmarks of the diocese. Now, under the conservative, judgmental, and passionless leadership of Thomas Olmsted, the Catholic church in Phoenix has the sympathy and concern of clergy and laity throughout the United States.

It was clear from his arrival that Thomas Olmsted had come to get rid of the agreement that the county attorney had made with the diocese, to get the state government out of the running of the church. I believe that the agreement was officially terminated, but I think the county still has great authority over the local Catholic church – far more than anybody is willing to admit.

It appears to me that Thomas Olmsted came to set things right in the minds of his superiors. So the Catholic church of Phoenix is very different today, with a different leadership and vision. And I think many of us are battered and scarred by what we went through. I know that I will never be the same.

Never in my wildest dreams did I expect to sit on a stand to testify about my beloved friend, Bishop O'Brien. Never in my wildest dreams did I expect to take a call on a cell phone from a papal nuncio to give me directions from the pope, and to have the painful details of that call scooped by a predatory press.

Never in my wildest dreams did I expect a good man like Bishop Thomas J. O'Brien to have his ministry torn apart by these kinds of catastrophic events.

However, I would soon encounter experiences that were equally as devastating.

CHAPTER 10
POPE BENEDICT XVI

People had been telling me for years that I needed to take some time off. It has been my tendency throughout my life to be something of a workaholic. So despite being difficult for me, the time off forced on me by being on administrative leave allowed me to learn to become more flexible and do things I wanted to do, as simple as they might be.

Right after the death of Pope John Paul II, I got a call from a buddy of mine named Jeff Berghoff. Jeff came all the way through the Life Teen program, and is now married and has a beautiful little girl. He's also a very successful landscape architect. He phoned and said, "Dale, let's go to Rome for the pope's funeral. I'll take you."

I said, "Jeff, I would love to go, but I'm going to Hawaii."

It sounded funny coming from me, but I had promised some friends I would go and be present for a wedding and I couldn't change my plans. So I said to Jeff, "You know, what might be even more exciting is to be in Rome when the new pope is elected."

He said, "Okay, great. Let's put that kind of trip together."

Knowing how the election of a new pope works, I sat down and counted out the days, and figured out when the cardinals would most likely be going into conclave, and what the greatest chance timewise would be to be at the Vatican when the new pope was elected.

We made arrangements to fly out of Phoenix on a Sunday morning, which with the time change would get us into Rome on Monday morning. There were four of us who were going. Besides Jeff and me, there was Lance Smaw who is a captain with the fire department and has multiple children, and Phil Calzadilla who has been a friend but not somebody I knew as well, and who is a wonderful man and a computer geek. I prepared to set out with three married men whose wives were all quite happy to see them having such an adventure, and who were probably looking forward to having the guys shipped out of the country for a few days.

We plotted everything out carefully, and despite the fact that there are many times in life that plans don't work out exactly as you make them, this time they all did. We arrived in Rome on Monday morning, got to the hotel, dropped off our stuff, and made it to the Vatican. We arrived in time to file past the gravesite of Pope John Paul II before the crowds got massive again, and we also arrived in time to see the cardinals go into conclave.

That was exciting in itself, but we were also there on Monday night when the first vote took place. When the smoke went up, the people started to cheer because it looked like it was white, but then it looked like it was black. It was hard to tell. But it turned out to be black. No pope.

So we left, had a nice dinner, went back to the hotel, and had a good night's sleep. The next morning we got up, and arrived at the Vatican in time for the second vote. The second batch of smoke was black; there was no doubt about it. It was Tuesday in the late morning.

We shopped, and did some of the tourist things you want to do at the Vatican, and Tuesday night we made plans to be there for the smoke signals which were supposed to occur at about seven o'clock.

We ate together in a café on one of the side streets, and as were walking back I said to the others, "I will meet you back in about an hour or so."

I wanted to look through the little gift stores and do some shopping, which I am prone to doing. We made arrangements to meet up in a little while and selected a spot to reconnect.

I arrived back a few minutes after the others, and as I approached the back of the plaza, I thought I saw smoke start to rise up. I couldn't really tell what the color was, and I couldn't determine if it was really smoke or a cloud behind the smoke stack. At first people were cheering, and then it was quiet, then bells started to ring but they were the six o'clock bells. Nobody knew what was going on.

Suddenly, the place just erupted, and there was no question that the smoke was white. Then the bells started to toll and noise came from everywhere.

I will never forget the scene. I was at the back of the plaza, and I could see down the side street, and people started running. They got out of their vehicles and left them in the street as they ran towards the plaza. The whole back side of the plaza was in motion, and it looked like the entire city of Rome was running. I heard later that people left their shops and hurried as fast as they could.

Everyone seemed aware that history was being made.

Because I was alone and was trying to get to the place where my friends had arranged to meet me, I was struggling with the crowd. The anticipation was intense as to who had been elected pope, and the excitement was literally electric.

Every time there was a movement at a window in the Vatican, the crowd would react. A simple ripple of a curtain, and the crowd cheered. It was a festival, an absolute celebration.

I had been to several World Youth Days, and this is what they had been like. People were singing, praying, and running. Nuns zipped by in their habits with their veils flying behind them.

Then, we saw workers come out and roll a huge banner over the railing on the balcony where the pope was going to appear. There were television cameras everywhere and tens of thousands of people jammed together shoulder to shoulder. You knew that the eyes of the world were on this one place at this one moment.

In the center of the plaza is an obelisk, a huge pillar that stands right in the middle. People clung to it to get a better view. Jeff was standing on a light pillar so he could see above the crowd. Then, cardinals began filing out onto the other balconies, which nobody remembered ever being done before.

The cardinal who was going to make the announcement came out, and again the crowd erupted. I was impressed with how many young people there were, how many languages were being spoken around me, and how many countries they represented. There were flags from all over the world – Africa, South America, Asia, you name it.

The cardinal spoke the ancient words, "Habemus papam," We have a pope.

Again, the place erupted.

"We have a pope." Four words are all it takes to change history.

As the cardinal began to read the proclamation, he said the name "Josef", and I didn't catch what that meant. The priest standing right next to me was German, and he started jumping up and down. He was elated. He said, "Josef, Josef, it's Ratzinger."

I thought to myself, "There's no way in the world the cardinals have elected Cardinal Ratzinger as pope."

But within seconds, it was announced that it was indeed Ratzinger, and that he was taking the name Pope Benedict XVI.

It was an amazing experience of the Catholic church. Even though there were many people in the crowd who really did not want Josef Ratzinger to be pope because of his conservative views, somehow in the moment all of that was suspended and the place just went crazy.

When Cardinal Ratzinger – now Pope Benedict XVI – walked out, he had the classic deer in the headlights look. You could see that the two people next to him, one being Bishop Marini, were telling him what to do, like "wave to the people."

The new pope was very awkward about how to respond to the crowd. When Pope John Paul II stepped out onto the balcony for the first time as pope, he took over the world. He may have been reluctant to be named the pope, but the moment he was elected, he became the pope completely. He knew what his destiny was.

In contrast, Pope Benedict XVI seemed willing to take on the job, but was uncertain as to what lay ahead. In the meantime, the crowd encouraged him, calling "Benedictus, Benedictus," the way they used to chant "JP 2, we love you."

Pope Benedict XVI was overwhelmed by the entire scene.

111

At this time, the Swiss Guard emerged. I must say, I wish that I was Swiss, better-looking, and thinner because they are very impressive. It would be a great gig to have.

Their uniforms were designed originally by Michelangelo, and added to the general pageantry and theatrical impact of the spectacle. A marching band even came through. Now I don't know how they managed to get an entire marching band in uniform, lined up, and ready to go in the space of time from the ringing of the bells to the announcement. I've been involved in parades, and they aren't something that just occur spontaneously. This band was perfection in the space of a half an hour.

So there was a band playing, the Swiss Guard was in fine form, the cameras flashed, and the new pope was trying to learn to wave to the crowd. It was an incredible historic moment.

Suddenly I thought to myself, "Someday people will be filing by his tomb, too." He had stepped into the history books with the other popes during that short walk to the balcony. I knew I would always remember that I was right there in the center of things when Benedict XVI gave his first papal blessing.

I got a call from some of the media in Phoenix to ask if I would do an interview. They had called my secretary in Phoenix to arrange it, and it turned out that the interview was set for 2:30 in the morning Rome time. My three traveling companions were just fabulous and refused to go back and go to bed, which would have been the reasonable thing to do. Instead, they said, "No, we're a team. We're going with you. If you're awake, we're awake."

Thank God they stayed with me, because we got thoroughly lost. The taxi driver was completely turned around, and we were at the Vatican plaza in the middle of the night trying to find the address. The satellite was supposed to come on at 2:30, and we arrived at 2:29 on a rooftop overlooking the Vatican. It was one of the most stunning sights I have ever seen in my life.

A woman walked up to me and said, "Have you met Larry King before?"

I said, "Uh, no."

She asked, "Do you need to talk to him before you go on the air?"

I said, "I don't think I'm here for Larry King. I am here for a local interview with Channel 3 in Phoenix."

So she escorted me to the tent that was next to the one where Larry King was going to conduct his interview. However, I had come perilously close to copying Pope Benedict XVI's deer in the headlights look. I did manage to connect with Channel 3 to talk to the people in Phoenix about the election of the new pope.

I know there are many people who struggle with the Catholic church's traditions and teachings, especially these days with the return to conservatism. But with the election of the new pope, the presence of the Holy Spirit transcended differences in cultures, languages, music, and opinions, at least for a little while.

One of my friends who is a doctor made the pragmatic statement, "I wouldn't expect Cardinal Ratzinger to be around very long. He's got that look that he's not doing very well."

So I don't know how long Benedict XVI will serve the Catholic church, but in some ways he may surprise everybody. I don't know what ultimately lies ahead for the pope, for the Catholic church, or for me. But I do know that being in that plaza at that moment was an unexpected surprise.

It is interesting that Benedict XVI is the one who laicized me – and supported Tom Olmsted in his excommunication of me. You would think someone who joined the Nazi party in his youth would be merciful towards other people and whatever their mistakes might be. But, I fear the "self-righteousness" of the Catholic church today is very alive and continues to impact how others are dealt with.

CHAPTER 11
THE LEGAL SYSTEM GOES BONKERS!

The most unexpected events of my life occurred right before Thanksgiving in 2005.

One morning, I walked out of my apartment to my car only to be greeted by two carloads of detectives waiting to arrest me. I was taken to the county jail, booked, and charged with 10 misdemeanors. I spent the day in jail before I had a hearing and was released into house arrest.

No one I consulted had ever heard of anyone being placed under house arrest for misdemeanor charges, but I believe the court commissioner, Barbara Hamner, was intimidated by the viciousness of the press broadcast media, and the general meanness of the county attorney's office in its dealings with me. She acted in a prejudicial and unfair manner. The county attorney requested house arrest because two other priests had fled the country.

Commissioner Hamner evidently felt I was somehow responsible for their actions, and I should be punished.

Since that November, I have been the unwilling subject of a great deal of press, much of it sensationalistic. I also incurred overwhelming legal expenses, which I had to absorb personally as my attorneys and I defended the charges against me.

Three charges were dropped. The other charges — which included contributing to the delinquency of a minor, indecent exposure, and assault — remained. There was great variance in opinion among the various attorneys as to the legal ramifications of these charges. Despite the more than 20-year lapse between the alleged events and allegations being made, a statute of limitations did not apply in Arizona.

I could defend myself in these next few paragraphs, but I will not. I will say only that I could never have expected anything like this.

After a few months, a justice of the peace removed the house arrest. I was grateful because it was one of the most difficult situations I had ever grappled with in my life. I spent Thanksgiving, Christmas, and New Year's in virtual solitary confinement.

The entire legal situation was made even more perplexing because it is played out before a justice of the peace who is not an attorney, and whose background in law is limited. In Arizona, a justice of the peace is required only to be a citizen who speaks English and is a high school graduate. However, I will state that the justice of the peace in Chandler, Arizona, made every effort to be fair and impartial.

After my arrest, it seemed that all I did was wrestle with God, waste time, and talk to attorneys. I have been told that the Diocese of Phoenix worked directly with the county attorney to destroy me. Although I tried to grasp the significance of the details as they were revealed to me, to this day I don't know what any of this means beyond the hurt and despair it has caused me, and those close to me.

I struggled with myself, the Catholic church, and my future. I went from working 80 hours a week performing meaningful service that I loved doing, to doing nothing of true substance other than surviving.

As a human being, I have made mistakes, which I freely admit and am willing to embrace as mine to rectify. As a person of faith, I also know that God's love is unconditional.

Mistakes do not muffle God's call or divert God's love. We are all the work of His hands.

I am stunned that the Catholic church — which was my ministry for decades and claims to be the body of Christ — was not even His face for me. On a purely human level, the Catholic church offered no sense of concern or caring, and certainly no gesture of support.

The county attorney, Andrew Thomas, and two of his assistants – Barbara Marshall and Lisa Aubuchon – pursued me as hard as possible. My attorneys and I eventually went to the Arizona Supreme Court twice to defend my rights. We prevailed both times.

At one point I was offered a plea bargain to end the ordeal. Barbara Marshall asked to meet with me, although it is unusual to have such a meeting. At the meeting, I asked why they were seeking to end their pursuit of me at this particular time. She said something I will never forget. She replied that they had only two goals. First, to remove me from the priesthood. Second, to hold me accountable in the court of public opinion through the media. (In other words, to embarrass me.) She said she and her colleagues never expected anything beyond that.

This of course represented an ethical violation and I believe that Thomas, Marshall, and Aubuchon should be disbarred for abuse of power. Interestingly enough, as of this writing Thomas and Aubuchon are currently under federal investigation for matters not related to my situation, and Marshall has been demoted. In fact, an investigator for the Arizona Supreme Court has recommended that Thomas and Aubuchon be disbarred.

During these months and years, the stress and anxiety were indescribable and overwhelming. Whenever I was in public, I feared the police, the media, and even people who used to be friends. I do not know how I survived. I was hurt, humiliated, and lost.

However, things only got crazier. The mother of one of the "victims" sent a request for me to visit her. She had recently learned she had cancer. Legally, I could not visit her. One day a letter came for me in the mail. She apologized to me and called the county agent a "scoundrel" for putting words in the mouths of my accusers. She asked me not to turn the letter over to the court – but said she did not want to die with this matter on her soul. She knew the truth. She asked me to talk to her son because she believed he had been molested.

I did as she requested. Years later, the county claimed I was trying to set the kid up.

Regardless, I do pray that this woman, who has now died, is resting in peace.

The media never let up. The Arizona Republic looked for every opportunity to repeat the same sordid yet inaccurate story over and over. Even when there was no news, they ran stories. Nobody ever had the insight as a true journalist to inquire as to how many hundreds of thousands of dollars of taxpayers' money was being wasted trying to find something to condemn me for. No one ever sought my account of the events.

In April 2010, Andrew Thomas resigned as Maricopa County Attorney to begin another campaign for public office. The day he departed, prosecutors offered a plea bargain to me. When it was all said and done, I pled guilty to one misdemeanor charge stemming from an incident in 1986, paid a $250 fine, and walked away from it all.

Although some of the media outlets portrayed my acceptance of a plea bargain as an admission of guilt, almost every thinking person saw through it. Five years? Two trips to the Arizona Supreme Court? Hundreds of thousands of dollars in tax money? Eight years of investigations, press conferences, media hype? Making accusations against me a higher priority than ongoing murder cases, including serial killers who terrorized the Valley? All for a $250 fine?

The bishop of the Phoenix Catholic diocese, Thomas Olmsted, did everything possible through his access to the media and through the nonprofit publication, The Catholic Sun, to taint whatever jury pool might eventually have been assembled. However, the case never went to a jury.

I am relieved these events are behind me. However, I will never recover. Since the beginning of the ordeal, hundreds of people – most of whom I have never met – have contacted me to express sorrow for my pain and relief that the curtain had finally fallen on the tragedy. I had not realized how much support I had.

The best way for me to end this section is to share with you the statement I made the Sunday after I accepted the plea deal, and the nightmare finally ended:

Just in the last few days, I can tell you, there is some light in my soul, some brightness in my heart, and hope in my voice. I trust many of you share those same feelings. My message today is simple. I want to say a total of seven words:

I love you

I'm sorry

Thank you

First, let me say to you, "I love you." Last week in our Gospel reading, Jesus asked Peter three times, "Peter do you love me?" And three times, Peter said, "Lord, you know I love you." Perhaps what we learn from that Gospel is that saying it one time is not enough. So I stand before you today, and I say,

I love you,

I love you,

I love you!

I will always be grateful to you for standing with me. The core members who helped start this community...those who have sacrificed special titles and places in other religious communities, and those who have given so freely of themselves – to all of you, I say:

I love you!

You have become the face of Christ for me. In moments, sometimes days of loneliness, your love was there. And today, I hope you hear in my words my love for you. In a country where a person is supposed to be innocent until proven guilty, it is clear to me that it is rare to find people, like you, who hold on to that value...and live it.

Second, I am sorry. I realize that over four decades of religious service I have hurt and offended others. Sometimes, it was a matter of perception or mis-perception...and sometimes it was my fault. But, no matter what caused it, I am truly sorry for any hurts. That being said, I need to say that despite my faults, I committed no crimes. I share something in common with all the citizens of

Maricopa County – my legal problems started the day Andrew Thomas took office and ended the day he left. My attorneys, Mike Manning and Tom Hoidal, have been tremendous. With their help, we decided to end this legal nightmare by admitting to a non-sexual action that happened 25 years ago. Going ahead with the trial would have been very difficult because I was unwilling to BREAK the seal of confession.

I don't remember the incident specifically, but sometime around 1985, I hit this young man in the groin area. It had become part of playing basketball with the teenage boys. I did not know he was offended, and a few years later, when he asked me to do his wedding and the baptism of his child he did not tell me he was offended. Nonetheless, I should not have taken part in that behavior; I was the adult. I often tried to just be "one of the guys" so that the kids would open up to me. It was my mistake. I am sorry. It certainly was not sexual in nature.

As you know, as of Thursday, April 15th, all the allegations of sexual misconduct have been legally dismissed. So...I ask forgiveness for creating this nightmare for so many and I ask forgiveness of God, for not being the man of love I should have been.

Third, I want to say thank you – to God for walking with me in this shadow of death, and to my mom and my family. They've showed what FAMILY truly is...a place of unconditional love. I want to thank all who prayed for me – thousands. People would come up to me in grocery stores and malls, and tell me they were praying. I want to thank all who continued to be a friend...no matter what others were saying...no matter what the cost. I want to thank you for the gift of the Praise and Worship Center. And I even want to say thank you for the pain. It has caused me to think more deeply and to become a more compassionate person. As a result of the pain, I will be a better person.

One of the great disappointments for me has been the lack of love and support I received from the church that I loved so dearly.

Bishop Olmstead forced me to look outside of the Catholic church for love and community. I have found just that, and have found that God's presence and truth is not limited to any ONE denomination – it is available to ALL.

The reading today finds the apostles looking up to heaven waiting for Christ to return. I can relate. For five years...I waited for Christ...I would wake up in the morning almost angry that I had to face another day. But God isn't finished with me yet. There is more work to do. And so, like the apostles of old, each of us here needs to hear the message...and get to work.

My first order of work is to forgive those who have hurt me, and to ask forgiveness of those I have hurt. It is the fundamental work of the gospel...RECONCILIATION.

My brothers and sisters, we live in difficult times. We have a political system that is not based on service; we have a justice system not based on truth; and we have a religious system not based on God's love. There is a lot for us to do.

I pledge to you my efforts to work hard to create a better place for us all. I ask you to continue to walk with me as we build the Praise and Worship Center – a place not created by accident or default – but by God's design.

Five years from now, we will look back...and praise the amazing God who has created a unique, wonderful, loving, inclusive, non-judgmental, Christ-based, Spirit-filled community. Stick with us...amazing grace is about to fall upon us all.

CHAPTER 12
PRAISE & WORSHIP CENTER

The Praise & Worship Center is a legal nonprofit organization founded in 2007. The mission of PWC is two-fold: to be a supplement to the spirituality of Catholics who are looking for a more dynamic community, and to serve as a full-service church for those who choose to make it their church "home."

The membership of PWC is a third, a third, and a third – one third practicing Roman Catholics who attend both regular Catholic mass, and PWC; one third ex-Roman Catholics who no longer choose to practice the Catholic faith; and one third who come from other or no faith backgrounds.

As I write this chapter, PWC has a facility, small staff, and a bright future. New ministries are beginning, and slow but steady growth has marked the past three years.

So – that's the objective description of the Praise & Worship Center. Now here's the real scoop, and the answers as to why the founding of the Praise & Worship Center led to my excommunication from the Catholic church.

Starting in 2006, I felt very isolated from the brotherhood of priests and the people I had served. Life Teen distanced itself from me. Staff members from the parish and the chancery were fearful of reaching out. Hundreds of members of St. Tim's wrote offering support, but weren't sure what to believe or what to do. I was grieving…and yet the basic Christian call to bring joy to those in sorrow never seemed to apply to me. I felt absolutely set adrift from everything I had known and loved.

I privately had mass with some good friends, Fred and Jean Bruno. They would have me to their home for breakfast and mass. As a few others heard about the gathering, requests to pray together started surfacing. That growing group turned into what would become a core group for the Praise & Worship Center.

At the same time, Mark Dippre was a constant support. Mark had been a priest and my associate at St. Tim's for more than five years in the late 1990s. While we worked together we laughed, we cried, and we labored extremely hard to grow the church. Mark left active ministry and married his best friend, Helen.

As a priest, Mark was often in trouble with church authorities for breaking one rule or the other. I often protected him. He would tease, "Let's start our own quasi-Catholic church!"

We would laugh, and he would say, "No rules!"

Mark and I worked well together. We also had a Lucy and Ethel relationship. When he joined our core group for the Praise & Worship Center, it was clear we were a team again and the dream of a "quasi-Catholic" community was born.

As we started, we were careful to not lead anyone away from the Catholic church. At the same time, church leaders were extremely threatened by our presence.

Thomas Olmsted, the bishop, put pressure on me to resign and to request to be laicized. There was no direct contact between us other than a few certified letters. I stopped receiving his letters after he sent one threatening me that if I wrote a book he would sue me. Meanwhile others at the chancery pressed me to resign and request laicization.

I was confused as to what to do. I initially agreed to request to be laicized until I was told that by requesting this, I was also agreeing to the consequence of excommunication if I performed ANY ministry. The thought of never again preaching, teaching, or visiting the sick was not an option. So – I decided to "pastor" the Praise & Worship Center. Mark Dippre decided to co-pastor and move forward with his life. The Praise & Worship Center core group courageously decided to create a place where EVERYONE was welcome to pray.

Our first service was held on Thanksgiving Day, 2007. Well more than 600 people showed up. The media was surprised, to say the least. The Catholic diocese was alarmed, and very angry. And the people were thrilled.

Some of the folks who came wanted to see me or have closure with me. Some came out of curiosity. Others came because they were spiritually hungry.

Since that first service, we moved to other quarters, and eventually landed at Fiesta Fountains, in Mesa, Arizona. Fred Bruno kept saying, "We need to have a weekly service."

He was right.

For the next several months, about 300 to 400 people showed up for services. Little by little, other ministries were launched. The music at worship got better and better. At one point, I asked the community if it was the right time to get our own facility. The vast majority of the congregation stood in support of the idea.

We laid out a five-month program to raise $90,000 for a facility fund. This money had to be over and above regular giving. In seven days we had $100,000 in pledges and gifts. It became clear to our community leaders that the support was there. After months of searching, we decided on a 12,000-square-foot building in Chandler, Arizona.

At the same time we were signing documents to lease this facility (April 2010), my legal situation concluded. Light started coming back into my soul. The building became a sign of HOPE to me.

Several months before I had received a phone call from Mark Dippre on a Monday morning. Mark had received a phone call from a priest saying the Catholic diocese had sent out an e-mail saying that Mark and I were excommunicated from the Roman Catholic church. I was driving to the office and turned the news on the radio and heard the same message. When I arrived at the office, I found two letters from Thomas Olmsted (one for me and one for Mark). Mark came into our tiny temporary office. He opened his letter. The truth is I never opened mine. I ripped it up and threw it away. I had decided that Tom Olmsted would have NO more power over me. As painful as this was, it was also freeing.

Again, the media went crazy. Friends wept. Some people were shocked. Others rejoiced that Mark and I were publicly "shamed."

Actually, I knew a little about the excommunication beforehand. At one point during one of the three conversations I had with Olmsted in five years, he told me outright that he had his canon lawyers looking for a reason to excommunicate me.

I could also have hired a canon lawyer, but my legal fees were already huge. The cost to defend myself in criminal court was $150,000. About a third of that came from a public defense fund, a third came from my mother, and a third came from me. I had NO money and little interest in hiring a canon lawyer to defend me in church courts. Besides, Olmsted was very powerful. And he was determined to excommunicate Mark and me.

Because of the excommunication, battle lines were drawn. Catholics became fearful of retributions from the Catholic diocese, or their local parish, if they were known to frequent the Praise & Worship Center. Fear becomes debilitating, and many people were terrified.

Several months after the excommunication, Olmsted announced that I had been laicized. He sent a priest friend with the paperwork. He offered to meet with me. I accepted the offer so I could say some things directly to him. Olmsted timed the announcement to influence the trial. However, the trial was never held. But he used the Catholic Sun newspaper to try to destroy me. So many facts recounted in the paper and that were cited in the laicization were lies. But, I was never asked to refute any of the accusations. And you know what? It doesn't really matter.

Excommunication is the Catholic death sentence. You are no longer even allowed to pray publicly in a Catholic church. The problem is that once the authority of the Catholic church excommunicates a person, there is nothing else they can do to him or her. And the simple truth is, church authorities do not control God.

"For I am convinced that neither death nor life, neither the present nor the future, nor any powers, neither height nor depth, nor anything else in creation, will be able to separate us from the love of God that is in Jesus Christ our Lord." (Romans 8: 38-39, NIV)

As of today, the people of Praise & Worship are under threat. Things are so polarized that an organization that I helped found (Paz de Cristo in Mesa, Arizona) in a building that I was instrumental in getting built sent us a letter saying that they will not accept gifts from PWC for the poor. They are willing to let others go hungry in order to be "righteous."

June 17, 2010

Dear Praise and Worship Center,

As many of you know, Paz de Cristo has a long history in the East Valley community and has been through many changes over the last few years. This includes achieving its independence to become its own Non-profit 501(c)3 agency. As a result of this, Paz de Cristo is in many ways a new organization working hard to establish additional partnerships and tap new funding sources that will secure a fruitful future for us.

In these hard economic times and in conjunction with our independence, much of our recent funding has come from grants and our faith-based partners who understand the importance of serving the hungry and providing basic needs. As we are promoting our awareness in the community as a stand alone [sic] Non-profit organization, we are faced with making decisions that will secure a sustainable future for us with faith-based organizations, foundations, donors at large.

The Board of Directors has become aware that there are controversies surrounding the Praise and Worship Center that could potentially jeopardize funding for Paz de Cristo. Therefore, the Board of Directors of Paz de Cristo feels that it is in the best interest of Paz to decline funding or donated goods from the Praise and Worship Center. Additionally, we ask that you refrain from using Paz de Cristo in your newsletters, other advertisements and media.

We hope that you can understand this difficult decision that we have had to make for the future of Paz de Cristo as we market and promote ourselves in the Valley. Thank you so much for all that you have done to support Paz in the past.

May the Peace of Christ shine upon you,
Sincerely,
(signed) Terrence P. Woods

President, Board of Directors

At this time, I choose to take the high road. I say little against the Catholic church, although I have what could be extremely damaging information. I do not want to hurt anyone's faith. But at the same time, I do not desire to stop serving God. And, I do not choose to allow others to destroy me.

The Gospel is about freedom. By Christ we are given the freedom to love, the freedom to be forgiven, and the freedom to be human.

Life is very different now, but it is good. I miss my former life, and I still feel like a priest. As someone told me, "I call you Father because it is a relationship, and not a title."

I still use the name "Fr. Dale" although I don't call myself "Monsignor Dale" (although others do). Some have said it's like calling an ex-governor by the name of "Governor" as a sign of respect for what they accomplished. And the simple fact is none of this matters to God. Love matters.

What we are doing at Praise & Worship is dynamic. It has the potential to grow tremendously. It also has the potential to fill a spiritual need of those inside and outside the Catholic church. I do know that God is present when we pray together. And I also know that the Praise & Worship Center will continue to be controversial.

But scripture gives us the true litmus test. "By their fruits you shall know them." The fruit of Praise & Worship Center has been to give life. Each person, and ultimately God, will have to judge the fruits of how the Catholic church is serving Christ's people.

I hope and pray that God will continue to teach us all how to forgive and love each other more deeply.

CHAPTER 13
THE HUMAN NEED FOR HOPE

I really wanted to end this book by talking about hope. Through the course of my life I have come to understand that hope is a basic human need. We were created in hope. When God created each of us, He had hope for us that we would spend eternity with Him. We all began the same, as the apple of His eye.

When we were born, there was hope that we would learn how to love, how to live, and how to take care of each other. It is still the basic desire of most parents when they gaze on their newborn children.

Hope is defined as expectation and desire combined. I think this is a marvelous definition. We not only expect something, but we desire for it to take place. On a shallow level, hope is something that we deal with every day. We go to a basketball game, and we hope our team wins. We raise our kids, and we hope that they will go out into the world and find what they are supposed to do with their lives.

We plan a picnic, and we hope that the weather will cooperate, and that the ants will leave us alone.

But on a much deeper level, there is hope that unites all human beings. I remember one Advent at St. Timothy's we picked as a theme, "Do Not Fear to Hope."

It was one of the most powerful Advents we ever observed, Advent being the time that we prepare for Christmas and the birth of Christ. We had signs up that said "Do Not Fear to Hope." We made banners, and sang songs with the same message.

We had kids in the religious education classes send cards to people in care centers and nursing homes. One of the kids wrote a beautiful card, and on the front he had written "Do Not Fear to Hope."

When you opened it up, it said, "Dear old person, Please don't die." And he signed it. I only hope that the person who received it still had a sense of humor. It has kept me laughing for years, I will freely admit.

Hope is something that kids have. They wake up in the morning and hope that it's going to be a good day. On a personal level, I know what it means to lose hope; I learned about living without it when I went through a serious depression.

I used to think that depression was caused by one of two things. I thought it was either a chemical balance, or was the result of a series of bad choices that had been made and the depressed person could just "choose" his way back out of it.

Certainly depression has those elements to it. Often there is a chemical imbalance involved. Unresolved issues, bad choices, and things that get inflicted on a person can all be factors. Depression brings about darkness, and it brings about a fear that literally becomes crippling on an emotional and a spiritual level.

Pope John Paul II wrote that courage is the basis for hope. I believe that to have hope in life you have to have the courage to face whatever is there – whether it's an outside enemy or an inside demon.

John Paul II faced communism and stared it down and lived in absolute hope that it would be defeated. Mother Teresa faced incredible odds of people dying in the streets, and had the courage to pick up one person and let that person die with dignity. With the death of that one person, the world became different.

I have come to understand that I must have courage to face myself, to face tomorrow, to face other people. But what is the basis of the courage that we need?

I think it's this: We need hope, and in order to truly have hope, we have to have the courage to accept love. That is the battle that most of us have our whole lives. We don't have the innocence and the guts to accept human or Divine love.

That's the human struggle.

Because what our real hope for is as human beings is acceptance. That is what unites every single human being. Rich people, poor people, sick people, healthy people, White people, Black people, young people, old people, gay people, straight people, married people, single people – we all just want to be accepted. Some people do go overboard and say, "This is who I am. I don't care what people think and I don't care if anybody likes me."

Nobody believes that rubbish. The person saying it doesn't really believe it, either. Deep down in the human heart is the hope that somebody will know us for who we really are and will still love us and accept us, and maybe even like us.

I am convinced that most teenage sex is part of a quest for acceptance. Young people – and not so young people – have become convinced that if you put your naked body next to somebody else's naked body, that you have experienced total acceptance. In some ways for an instant maybe you have. But in the next instant a guy can pull his pants up and walk away, a woman can stand up and get dressed, and then those two people may never see each other again.

A lot of drinking is done to do away with inhibitions. Some people drink to cover up their feelings of insecurity, or to forget their pain of rejection for awhile. People desire in the depths of their hearts to be a part of a larger whole, to be accepted.

In the mid-1990s, I had the honor of being appointed by the governor of Arizona to be one of the representatives of the state of Arizona at the Summit on America's Future that was held in Philadelphia. It was a star-studded gathering, to be sure. It was hosted by Colin Powell, who is truly an amazing man, and there was a cast of thousands. Or at least hundreds.

All of the living presidents were invited and all were present, with the exception of Ronald Reagan who was already too ill to attend. However, Nancy Reagan appeared on his behalf and was very gracious.

I was on the tenth row as the presidents were speaking, and it was a unique show of power. I shook hands with George and Barbara Bush, and with Jesse Jackson who was not at all impressed with my Roman collar, let me assure you.

The whole focus of this gathering was about mentoring, and how young people need to be mentored into the people they are supposed to be, and that mentoring would guarantee our future as a country.

They were trying to line up literally thousands of people to do hundreds of thousands of hours of community service to mentor our youth. As somebody who has worked with young people for decades, I was inspired by that goal, and I was encouraging of it. But despite the glitter, I was left cold by what I saw.

When the whole event was over, there seemed to be big hole in it. I am not just spiritualizing when I say that it was a completely secular experience. It was good, and the goals were lofty, but it was not fulfilling on a deeper level.

Mentoring somebody in an area of his or her life will never replace loving somebody and accepting them for what they are. So it's a good thing to mentor somebody, and if you're a good athlete it's a fine thing to help somebody else build his or her confidence. If you're a musician, it's a great thing to encourage someone else coming up behind you. But mentoring never replaces the human need to be known, to be loved, and to be accepted.

That is really what our human journey is about. Think of somebody lying on a deathbed. What does he want? He fears letting go, because he doesn't know what is on the other side.

I believe that the more convinced you are that there is love and acceptance on the other side, the more gracefully and grace-filled you will drown. People on their deathbeds want to be accepted by God, even though they may have really messed up royally at some point in their lives.

Often people reveal terrible secrets as they are dying. They let go of whatever they have been hiding, perhaps for their entire lives. They need in their final breaths to hear somebody say, "You are forgiven. You are accepted. You are loved. You are rescued."

What does a couple want from marriage? Each person wants the same thing from the other – to be known and accepted.

There are all kinds of other dynamics that might shape a marriage – careers, material desires, ambitions – but when the basic elements of understanding and acceptance aren't there, nothing else works. The marriage is empty, and probably a temporary arrangement.

What happens at confession? I remember as a young priest coming out of mass and encountering a girl dragging two boys by their hands. The closing song was still going on, but she was out that door and cornered me saying, "These guys need to go to confession."

I said, "Okay, but do they want to go to confession?"

She said, "Yes."

I said, "Okay, why don't you just stand off to the side so I can greet people, and then I will be glad to hear their confessions."

She said, "Please, don't make them wait. They need to go now."

So I took the first kid in, and it was really a beautiful exchange. He was 17 years old, and hadn't been back to confession since he had made his first one almost 10 years before. Then the second kid came in, and for literally 45 minutes he wept. My vestments were covered with his snot, and he cried and had his head in my lap, and hiccupped.

At the end of it, he looked up and wiped the tears from his eyes and said, "Now I know why you Catholics go to confession."

I said, "You Catholics? Aren't you Catholic?"

He said, "Oh no, but my friends told me that this was really good."

I've made mistakes in my life. And I don't ever want to say that I am glad for them, but they certainly have made me a better person and a better pastor. I have come to see that God sees through all our human failings and still loves each of us. Divine love is something that is never deserved, and cannot be earned. It is a gift.

We have to learn to know ourselves, and, yes, we have to work on getting rid of the bad elements of our lives, and perhaps go to counseling to wade through the mud that sometimes pours over our doorsills. But when it's all said and done, it does not change the fact that we were created in hope.

It's a hope that will not leave us empty. It is a hope that will leave us absolutely fulfilled.

The greatest gift we can give to our family, our friends, to the ones with no hope, and to each other is to accept each other. Sometimes when you do that people criticize you and say, "You're accepting their bad behavior, their sinfulness."

That doesn't make any sense. It makes God look bad when someone insists on maintaining this view, on citing some rulebook instead of being the face of Christ for another person.

God doesn't accept hatred. He doesn't accept negativity and sin. But He accepts us. That is the reason we can all say, "Do not fear to hope."

We were created to accept love.

In my whole five-year ordeal, I prayed for hope. One of the most painful elements of my experience was when a great friend of mine went to the diocese and told the officials that she believed I was without hope and suicidal. I knew I was in a deep depression, but I did not know how obvious it was. Nobody from the diocese ever reached out to me in any way. Thomas Olmsted, the bishop, never called. The vicar of priests, who has now been appointed as a bishop, never called. In fact, when I called him for help, he never returned my call. I believe in my heart of hearts that Tom Olmsted hoped I would end my own life. Although he is wildly anti-abortion, he certainly had no respect for my life.

137

It was a few people – most of whom I would never had expected to rally behind me – who became HOPE for me. I pray I can return the favor by being hope for someone else.

Resurrection and restoration are marks of our God. Without getting all preachy – I would say they are also the marks of God's people.

I am finding hope. I am finding laughter. I am not suicidal. I am ALIVE again.

CONCLUSION

One of my favorite sayings is, "This, too, shall pass."

When I was younger, I thought this scripture reminded us that the storms of life pass away. I was sure that it meant that we should not focus on the negative because it will not last. In my "maturity" I have learned what God is really saying is: EVERYTHING passes away. EVERYTHING in this life ends. Jody Serey, my co-writer, was the first to tell me this truth.

I have had incredible highs in my life. I have also had lows beyond what I can describe. And the truth is, it all passes. The moments of "notoriety" in the Arizona Republic for helping to bring the Pope and Mother Teresa to Phoenix passed, and eventually turned into months of notoriety because of the clergy sex scandal. And eventually, this too shall pass. And by the way, so will the Arizona Republic. So will I. So will you.

In the midst of all of the unexpected events of life, my mom, dad, sister, and brother have stood by me. My father passed away. But, the love of family and some friends has been a gift. The love of some friends passed away when my position passed away and I could no longer "do" for them what they wanted or needed. Others have remained as a great sign of hope.

I do not want this book to end on a mushy spiritual note with a bunch of clichés about God and His goodness. I have two master's degrees in theology and I often don't have a clue where God is and why some things happen.

I do know that I have come to expect the unexpected. And the most unexpected gift in my unexpected life is God's unconditional love. Everything but this will pass away.

Today, most folks still call me "Fr. Dale." I am pastor of a multi-denominational church, and I am rebuilding my life. Some say they are shocked because I was "so Catholic" and had such a great faith in the eucharist. But, no one who really knew me is surprised. They knew I would not stay down forever. When your "spouse" of four decades divorces you, you grieve, hurt, cry, and then try to survive. I will always love the Catholic church – but I am not in love with her any longer.

At some point, especially in a crisis, one has to make a decision to either listen to the voice within, or the voices from the outside. The outside voices kept telling me that I was DONE, that I was HATED, and that I am not worthy enough to even sit in a pew in a Roman Catholic church to pray.

The voice within tells me I am loved, and God isn't finished with me yet. I now clearly choose to heed the inner voice. I believe it is of God.

Milestones

1952	Born in Cleveland, Ohio
1970	Graduated from Phoenix Central H.S.
	Entered St. John's Seminary, Camarillo, CA
1978	Ordained a priest, Diocese of Phoenix
	Appointed associate pastor, St. Jerome's Phoenix
1984	Master's degree in liturgy, University of Notre Dame
1985	Appointed pastor, St. Timothy's, Mesa, AZ
	Founded Life Teen Program
1987	Coordinator, mass with Pope John Paul II, ASU stadium, Tempe, AZ
1988	Founded Paz De Cristo Community Center, Mesa, AZ
1989	Coordinator, visit of Mother Teresa of Calcutta, Phoenix, AZ
1990	Received Pope Paul VI award for evangelization in the United States
1994	Coordinator, 25th anniversary, Diocese of Phoenix
1999	Coordinator, Millennium, Diocese of Phoenix

2000	Appointed Vicar General, Diocese of Phoenix
2001	Invested as Monsignor (Prelate of Honor) Founded St. Timothy's Catholic Academy
2003	Project coordinator, Diocesan Pastoral Center, downtown Phoenix ($15M project) Bishop Thomas J. O'Brien resigned as Bishop of Phoenix
2005	Resigned as pastor, St. Timothy's, Mesa, AZ
2005	Charged with misdemeanor "crimes" by Maricopa County Attorney, Andrew Thomas
2007	Began core group of Praise and Worship Center
2008	Praise & Worship Center begins holding services
2009	Excommunicated from the Roman Catholic church by Thomas Olmsted
2010	Paid $250 fine for one 25-year old misdemeanor; all other charges and sexual allegations dropped by Maricopa County
2010	Praise & Worship Center opens new facility in Chandler, Arizona

Breinigsville, PA USA
11 February 2011
255311BV00001B/3/P